STONES, BRICKS, AND HISTORY

The Corner of "Duke & George"

1798 – 1984

THE NORTH-EAST CORNER OF
ADELAIDE STREET EAST and
GEORGE STREET, TORONTO

Sheldon and Judy Godfrey

LESTER
&ORPEN
DENNYS
P U B L I S H E R S

Canadian Cataloguing in Publication Data

Godfrey, Sheldon J., 1938 —
   Stones, Bricks, and History

Bibliography: p.
ISBN 0-88619-070-3

1. Toronto (Ont.) - Streets -
Adelaide St. - History.
2. Toronto (Ont.) - Streets - George
St. - History.
3. Toronto (Ont.) - Buildings -
History. 4. Historic buildings -
Ontario - Toronto. I. Godfrey,
Judy, 1940 — II. Title.

FC3097.67.G62 1984 971.3′541
C84-098737-4
F1059.5.T6875A34 1984

This edition of this book has been
expanded and revised. Earlier
versions have been published under
different titles as follows:

   1st. edition: The Bank of Upper
Canada (August, 1979)

   2nd. edition: 252 Adelaide Street
East, A Profile in Architectural
History (February, 1980)

   3rd. edition: The Corner of Duke
& George (December, 1981)

PRINTED IN CANADA

PREFACE

For over one hundred and fifty years, the buildings on the north-east corner of Adelaide Street East and George Street in Toronto have witnessed a change in their immediate surroundings from muddy village to great metropolis and a change in their wider environment from a collection of colonial settlements to a great nation.

The Bank of Upper Canada Building, right on the corner, with its portico and stone columns, was significant architecturally throughout its existence. It provides examples of the 19th-century architectural styles of William Warren Baldwin, Francis Hall, John George Howard, Frederick William Cumberland and Henry Langley. It is the oldest surviving bank building in Canada.

By the 1970s, no one remembered who its architects were. No one would have known anything of the significance of the four other buildings which adjoined it - but for a plaque which announced that one of the structures had been built as the De La Salle School in 1871. No one had remembered that the bricked-up grey wing at the east end had been Toronto's first post office and is, in fact, the oldest surviving post office building in the country.

Of course, buildings owned by governments sometimes are well researched. All levels of government in this country have been known to cover the cost of studies to determine the architectural and historical background of buildings they own in order to determine whether spending public money on restoration is justified.

Not so with the private sector which has neither the financial nor the human resources to undertake that kind of feasibility study.

What follows in this book is a remarkable story about one group of buildings, the people who used them, and many of the events that took place there. Taken together, the buildings, the people and the events provide a window on the epic story that is part of our past since the early years of the last century.

What is even more remarkable is that this is only one story. There are many, many stories about other buildings in Canada just as significant in relation to their communities. If no one asks governments to put a priority on researching the background of privately owned buildings, those stories will never be written.

As must appear by now, this is not a book about history in any academic sense. It is about something tangible - a group of buildings that still exist and are still used. It is about touching something, wondering what has happened to it before, and seeing how it touches us as a community. History from this perspective is for all of us across the country who search for a tangible demonstration of what we have in common as Canadians.

Sheldon J. Godfrey
Toronto, March, 1984

Portico detail, 1979, before restoration

THE HISTORICAL CONTEXT: A VISIBLE LINK WITH THE PAST

The buildings at the north-east corner of Adelaide Street East and George Street date back to the early years of the last century.

Town Lot No. 6 on the north side of Duke Street, containing 9/10 of an acre, was laid out as the Town of York's first burial ground in 1798 although it may never have been used for that purpose. In 1806 it was patented to the Roman Catholic congregation for use as a chapel and there is evidence that a small building on the lot was destroyed during the War of 1812.

The stone building on the corner of Duke Street (now Adelaide Street East) and George Street served as the head office for the Bank of Upper Canada from 1827 to 1861.

The bank was the first chartered in Upper Canada in 1822 and was, in fact, the only bank in the province for more than ten years thereafter. The majority of its directors were members of the ruling clique or "Family Compact" that dominated the political life of the province. The bank was the sole financial agent for the provincial government during most of this period and its economic power was so great that it was the object of attacks by William Lyon Mackenzie and the Reformers and was the setting for one of the first incidents in the 1837 rebellion.

The red brick wing at the east end of the structure was originally built in 1833 to become Toronto's first post office. After the incorporation of Toronto in March, 1834, it was the only post office in Toronto until 1839, as well as being the residence of James Scott Howard, York's third postmaster (and Toronto's first), and Charles A. Berczy, the fourth postmaster.

An addition to the bank was built along George Street in 1851 and served as residence for Thomas G. Ridout, the bank's cashier or general manager.

After the failure of the Bank of Upper Canada in 1866, the bank and its addition were used by Mrs. Olive Stewart's Ladies Boarding School until the property was transferred to the Ontario government in 1870 by the bank's trustees. The buildings were purchased from the government by the Christian Brothers in November, 1870, equipped as a school and renamed the De La Salle Institute.

A further addition to the school was built between the bank building and the post office building in 1871.

In 1884 the property was transferred to the Board of Trustees of the Roman Catholic Separate Schools of Toronto. From that date it was used for varying periods of time for the De La Salle School, St.

Michael's School, and the Girls' High School, as well as serving as the board room and offices of the Catholic Separate School Board itself until the beginning of the new century.

In the face of constant criticism of the Catholic teachings of the Christian Brothers by Ontario school officials "if they had the least French accents", the Christian Brothers satisfied the requirements for English-speaking teachers by establishing a Novitiate, or teacher's academy, which operated from the De La Salle School building until May 1916.

After that date the building was used as a Royal Air Force recruiting centre for the First World War effort. In 1921 it was sold by the Catholic Separate School Board to Christie Brown & Company Limited, owners of the large biscuit plant on the south side of Duke Street.

Farmers' organizations, which had held political power through the United Farmers of Ontario government of E.C. Drury from 1919 to 1923, had consolidated their economic position through the widespread use of co-operatives. In October, 1925 the United Farmers Co-operative Co. Ltd. purchased the building on Duke Street from Christie Brown & Company Ltd., for use as a head office, a central storehouse and creamery.

The property was again sold on the 31st day of May, 1956 and was operated by Export Packers Company Limited as an egg packing plant until 1973.

Even in its declining industrial years, the bank building still served as an inspiration. In the 1960s and early 1970s, the upper floors of the bank building were rented to a number of artists who were later to achieve wide recognition. Michael Hayden, whose "Arc en Ciel" fluorescent sculpture later adorned the Yorkdale subway station in Toronto, developed his art in the Bank of Upper Canada building.

From 1973 the building was left unoccupied, except for the occasional transient, until a serious fire on June 30, 1978 opened it to the elements. The Bank of Upper Canada building had been declared a National Historic Site by the federal government in 1977 and designated to be of architectural and historic importance by the provincial government in 1975 — but its future was in jeopardy. "The building is worth saving for its architecture alone, but its history is even more important," wrote Donald Jones in the *Toronto Star* immediately after the fire. "The building is simply too important to be allowed to decay any further."(1)

---

(1) Donald Jones, "Town of York's last original building threatened". *Toronto Star*, Saturday, July 15, 1978.

THE CHURCH LOT

There is evidence that a small wooden building owned by the Catholic Church was the first building at the corner of Duke and George Streets.

In the early part of the year 1806, the Reverend Alexander Mac-Donell, the only Catholic priest in Upper Canada (later to become the first Catholic bishop in the province), left his parish of St. Raphael near Glengarry on the Lower Canadian border for a "tour through the upward parts of this province". In May, on his return, he reported to his superior the Right Reverend J.O. Plessis, Bishop of Quebec, that the Town of "York and its neighbourhood" had a Catholic population of 37 people, many of whom "had never seen a priest":

> Agreeable to your Lordship's request, I have got deeds made out for town lots in York and Kingston alloted for the use of Catholic Chapels and clergymen.

> The Deeds are made out in trust, that of York in the name of the Honourable James Babee [sic], Alexr. MacDonell, Speaker to the house of Assembly who is a Catholic, John Small Esq., and myself...The full fees for those two deeds should be fourteen pounds five shillings Halifax currency, but from personal con-siderations the President [Alexander Grant], Attorney General [Thomas Scott], and Receiver General, [Peter Russell] were so good as to remit their share of the fees which reduced the sum to ten pounds seventeen shillings and six pence currency.(1)

"Lot number six on the corner of George and Duke Streets in the Town of York", containing 9/10 of an acre, was granted by letters patent from the Crown to the four trustees on March 28, 1806, "in trust for the Congregation of Roman Catholics for the purpose of Erecting a Chapel for Public Worship". The grant added the proviso that "a good and sufficient dwelling house" should be erected upon some part of the land within one year.(2)

In July 1807 the Catholics of the Town of York met at the house of one of their number for the purpose of organizing themselves as a congregation. They elected elders authorized to collect money, and resolved "That as soon as sufficient funds may be found a Chapel shall be erected in the Town of York".(3)

While there are no available documents to describe the construction of the building, history records not only that a building was erected on the land but also that it was used during the War of 1812.

Years later, in 1870, the Archbishop of Toronto, Archbishop

Bishop Alexander MacDonell
(1762 — 1840)
Courtesy Metropolitan Toronto Library Board

(1) Rev. Alexander MacDonell to Bishop J.O. Plessis, May 10, 1806. *Plessis Papers.* Archives de l'Archevêché de Québec (AAN).

(2) Patent for Town Lot No. 6, on the corner of George & Duke Streets in the Town of York dated March 25th, 1806. Official Documents office, Ontario Ministry of Government Services.

(3) Resolution at a meeting of the Catholics of the Town of York held in the home of Dr. James Glennon, on July 13, 1807; *Plessis Papers*, loc. cit. reprinted in Edith G. Firth, *The Town of York 1793-1815* (The Champlain Society: University of Toronto Press, 1962) p.105.

(4) Archbishop Lynch to Bishop of London, Toronto, December 3, 1870. *Lynch Papers*, Archives of the Archdiocese of Toronto.

(5) MacDonell to Plessis, Glengarry, U.C., March 24, 1811, *Plessis Papers*, loc. cit.

(6) *See* "The Glengarry Light Infantry Fencible Regiment 1812-1816" by L. Summers & René Chartrand. *Military Uniforms in Canada, 1665-1970* (Canadian War Museum Historical Publication No.16, 1981).

(7) War of 1812, Claims for compensation No.334 and enclosure. R.G. 19, E 5(a) 3745, PAC. The claim for compensation for losses during the War of 1812 by Alexander MacDonell, York, for a house in York includes the following memorandum:
"D. Cameron [The Provincial Secretary] says he was surprised at the Church for seeking compensation for this house & does not know that it was habitable for some years before it was so burnt; was not here when burnt."
A search of Alphabetical Index in the City of Toronto Registry Office (Microfilm) does not reveal other land owned either by the Church, or by Alexander MacDonell as trustee for the Church, during this period.

(8) The Statute 29 Geo IV (1821) c.29 entitled "an Act to empower certain Trustees therein mentioned, to sell and convey a certain lot of land in the Town of York, and to Purchase another lot or Tract of Land for the Use and Accommodation of a Roman Catholic congregation."

(9) James Baby to Bishop MacDonell, York, February 1, 1824. Quoted in Edith G. Firth, *The Town of York, 1815-1834*, vol.2 (The Champlain Society, Toronto, 1966) p.187. See also Deed to William Campbell, registered 25 January, 1822 as Number 4114 for the County of York in the City of Toronto Registry Office.

Lynch, wrote to the Bishop of London referring to the lot which the Bank of Upper Canada had occupied at the corner of Duke and George Streets. "The lot had on it," he said, "over 50 years ago a small wooden church. Msgr. McDonald [sic] exchanged it for ten acres where St. Paul's and the House of Providence stand now."(4)

The exact use of the building during the period before the War of 1812 has not been documented, but it is possible at least that the Rev. MacDonell had the wooden building constructed as his residence in York. In March 1811, he wrote to his superior in Quebec requesting reimbursement for "my own expenses for 5 years between this [Glengarry] and Kingston and York upon the business of the Church where I have been obliged to remain for months supporting myself all the time without the aid of a single dollar from the good Catholics of those places".(5)

After the burning of Fort York in April of 1813, soldiers were billeted in unused structures in different parts of the town. A detachment of Glengarry Fencibles was in the building during the campaign of 1814.

The Glengarry Light Infantry Fencibles had been organized in Scotland of Catholic Highlanders by Rev. Alexander MacDonell and served in Ireland in 1798. In 1804, after the regiment was disbanded MacDonell came to Canada with several hundred Highlanders and took up land in Glengarry County in Upper Canada. Reorganized again in 1811, it was the only regiment of Upper Canada soldiers taken on as part of the regular British military establishment during the War of 1812 — the bulk of the Upper Canadian forces being constituted of local militias.(6)

As they were well trained, the Glengarrys were divided into small groups and used as a core for militia units in different parts of the province. A group of sixty Glengarrys was present at the surrender of Fort York in April 1813. In 1814, the Glengarry Fencibles were present at the battles of Lundy's Lane and Fort Erie.

A few hours after the Glengarry Fencibles left the house at the corner of Duke and George Streets during the winter of 1814, it was destroyed by a fire which was found to have been caused by the carelessness of the detachment.(7)

By 1822 the Catholic population of York and neighbourhood had increased to more than a thousand people and the trustees of the church lot at Duke and George Streets found it was "insufficient and inconvenient" for building a chapel.(8) After several months of negotiation the lot was sold for £250 in January 1822 to Sir William Campbell, whose house was under construction on the adjoining lot to the east. The money realized by the trustees from the sale was used toward the purchase of a 10-acre parcel on Power Street and the Catholic congregation had built St. Paul's Church by 1824.(9)

Private, Glengarry Light Infantry, 1813

BANK OF UPPER CANADA

From a woodcut by Thomas Young, 1850. Courtesy Public Archives of Canada

THE BANK OF UPPER CANADA BUILDING

On February 28, 1825, the Bank of Upper Canada purchased the lot at the corner of Duke and George Streets from the Hon. William Campbell for £500.(1)

The bank had been incorporated in 1821 and opened for business in 1822. It was to be the only bank in Upper Canada for ten years and the major bank the next forty. One quarter of its shares were owned by the government of the province, the balance by the ruling clique, popularly known a few years later as the "Family Compact". Nine of its fifteen original directors held appointed government positions.(2)

Almost from the outset the directors divided themselves into two groups. On one side was the "government party" or "court party", who became immortalized as the "Family Compact" by the 1830s. This faction was led by the Boulton, Robinson and Jarvis families, and the Anglican archdeacon, John Strachan.(3) On the other side were the moderates, mostly merchants or professionals led by the Baldwin and Ridout families. The distinctions were frequently blurred as almost all of the directors at some time or other held appointed government office and as some, such as William Allan, the bank's first president, did not at first belong to either party.

On April 7, 1825, less than six weeks after the Bank of Upper Canada had bought its land at Duke and George Streets, the *Colonial Advocate* remarked that the plans for the bank's new head office anticipated a front of hewn stone with the main body of brick. "It is thought by some", the editor noted, "that this bank, will be the finest public building in Upper Canada".(4)

Tradition has credited W.W. Baldwin with being the architect of the bank based on the statement in Rowsell's *Toronto City Directory*,

Dr. William Warren Baldwin
(1775 — 1844)

Courtesy Metropolitan Toronto Library Board

1850-51 that "we believe the building was designed by the Right Hon. Dr. Baldwin". Dr. William Warren Baldwin (1775-1844) had come to York in 1802. From 1803, "he practised medicine, law and occasionally architecture".(5) He served in the Legislative Assembly of the Province of Upper Canada during the 1820s.

It is likely that Dr. Baldwin had at least responsibility as a consultant for the plans of the bank's new head office. The plans were, by all accounts, initiated by Thomas Gibbs Ridout, the bank's cashier or general manager. Ridout was linked to Dr. Baldwin philosophically

(1) Deed from William Campbell to the Bank of Upper Canada dated February 28, 1825 and registered April 4, 1825 as No. 5165 for the County of York in the City of Toronto Registry Office.

(2) Adam Shortt, "The Early History of Canadian Banking", *Journal of The Canadian Bankers Association*, Vol. v (1897), p.21. For other articles on the incorporation of the bank, See Edwin C. Guillet, " Pioneer Banking in Ontario: the Bank of Upper Canada 1822-1866", *The Canadian Banker*, Vol. LV(1948) pp. 185-204, and Carol Lawrie Vaughan. "The Bank of Upper Canada in Politics, 1817-1840." *Ontario History*, Vol. 60 (1968) pp. 185-204.

(3) John Strachan (1778-1867) was born in Aberdeen and educated at the Universities of Aberdeen and St. Andrews. He came to Upper Canada in 1799 and taught at Kingston. In 1803 he was ordained priest in the Church of England and was appointed to Cornwall. While there he also ran a school which many boys from York attended. In 1812 he moved to York as minister of St.

James' and master of the Home District Grammar School, giving up the latter post in 1823 when he was appointed General Superintendent of Education for Upper Canada. In 1827 he became Archdeacon of York and first president of King's College, and in 1839 first bishop of Toronto. A member of the Executive Council, 1817-36, and the Legislative Council, 1820-41, he was one of the most powerful men in Upper Canada during the 1820's. Strachan was elected as a first director of the Bank of Upper Canada in 1822 and maintained his interest in bank affairs thereafter. See: Edith G. Firth, *The Town of York 1815-1834*, Vol. 2; (The Champlain Society, Toronto, 1966) p.8.

(4) *Colonial Advocate* (York), Appendix, 7 April 1825. "Increase of Private and Public Buildings"

(5) Eric Arthur, *Toronto No Mean City* (University of Toronto Press, Second edition 1974), Appendix A, p.224.

and by family ties. Dr. Baldwin became his uncle upon Ridout's marriage to Louisa Sullivan on April 5, 1825.(6) Besides, Dr. Baldwin, being in a community that had no resident professional architects, considered building an avocation and had some experience in design. Ridout considered the house that Baldwin had built for Quetton St. George as "by much the best and handsomest" in York, and perhaps in the province.(7)

Even more likely is the possibility that the architect originally engaged for the bank building was also its contractor, Francis Hall.(8) Hall (1792-1862) was a trained architect, born in Scotland, who had studied for about ten years in the office of the great architect and engineer Thomas Telford. Hall emigrated to Queenston, U.C., and in 1824 designed and constructed the monument to Sir Isaac Brock. By April 1825 he had, in partnership with Duncan Kennedy, secured the contract to construct the Bank of Upper Canada building under the name of Hall, Kennedy & Co.

Plans for the new bank as well as the contract with Hall, Kennedy & Co. had been authorized by the bank's cashier, Thomas G. Ridout and a group of directors he consulted. By early May, 1825, Ridout had arranged for the drilling of a well and the making of 200,000 bricks.(9) The foundation stone was to be laid by the end of that month.(10)

When the remaining government party directors heard of Ridout's initiatives they wrote to shareholders throughout the province accusing "the Cashier and Friends" of having solicited proxies "to insure the election of Dr. Baldwin as *President* of the Bank".(11) By the time of the annual election of the Board of Directors early in June, 1825, the government party had obtained sufficient proxies, mainly from the Niagara area, to increase their control of the Board. They were vocal in their opposition to the planned construction at Duke and George Streets.

"The Boultons and Robinsons wanted to abort the whole matter & get it erected on some lot up in the new Town" wrote John S. Baldwin to his partner in Montreal. "To effect this thing they managed the matter very cleverly and have completely out generalled us in the election....So that I fear the Boultons and Robinsons will have everything their own way which I am sorry for ... out of six Baldwins and Ridouts not one of them is in or even a friend of theirs."(12)

The resulting alterations in the plans caused great difficulty for those called upon to execute them. Hall, Kennedy & Co. was succeeded as contractor (probably in early 1826 when Francis Hall moved to Nova Scotia) by Kennedy, Kidd & Co., a partnership including Duncan Kennedy, John Kidd and Peter MacArthur. The new partners were all recent immigrants, unaware of the pitfalls when the bank directed a change in the specifications from brick to cut stone. "From information hastily collected," one of the contractors recalled later, "we were led to believe that stone of a proper quality could be procured at a much lower rate, than actually turned out to be the case; and we soon discovered that to continue the work under such circumstances was to incur certain loss."(13)

The contractors actually stopped work in 1826 but finally concluded they had no alternative but to finish in order to obtain some payment from the bank.(14) By the time the bank opened for business during the week of March 22, 1827,(15) Kennedy, Kidd & Co. had realized a loss of over £1,000.(16)

Although the portico with its sandstone columns and iron guard rail was not added until the 1840s, the bank's new head office was an imposing addition to York's public buildings of the 1820s. "The bank

(6) See "Thomas Gibbs Ridout", *Dictionary of Canaian Biography* (University of Toronto Press, Toronto, 1976),Vol. IX pp.661-663. See also: John Spread Baldwin to Julius Quesnel, March 31, 1825, "My niece Louiza Sullivan who used formerly to live with us to be married on Monday next to Mr. Thos. G. Ridout, the cashier of the Bank." *Quesnel papers*, Archives Nationales de Québec, (ANQ).

(7) Dr. W.W. Baldwin supervised the construction of Quetton St. George's house at the corner of King and Frederick Streets in 1810. See Edith G. Firth, *The Town of York 1794-1815*, Vol. I. (The Champlain Society, Toronto, 1962) pp. XXVII and 276. The quotation is from T.G. Ridout to Thomas Ridout his father, July 1811. R.M. & J. Baldwin, *The Baldwins and the Great Experiment*, (Longmans, Toronto, 1969) p.87.

(8) Stephen Otto, *Francis Hall*, (Town of York Historical Society, Toronto, 1983).

(9) On May 2, 1825, Thomas G. Ridout, Cashier of the Bank of Upper Canada, arranged for James Hopkins to make 200,000 bricks for the Bank building in the King's Park adjoining the Town. See Public Archives of Canada, RGS-AI Vol.72 p.38244.

(10) "Upper Canada Bank - The foundation stone of this elegant structure will be laid in a few days" *Colonial Advocate (York)*, May 23 1825.

(11) Strachan to Macaulay, May 30, 1825, *Macaulay Papers*, PAO MS78.

(12) John S. Baldwin, York, to his partner, Jules Quesnel, Montreal, June 9, 1825, *Quesnel Papers*, Archives Nationales du Québec, (ANQ).

(13) Petition of Peter MacArthur to the President and Directors of the Bank of Upper Canada, June 17, 1834. *Samuel P. Jarvis Papers*, F-125 B-67. Baldwin Room, Metropolitan Toronto Library Board. See also, *Colonial Advocate*, August 9, 1827.

(14) See Appendix I, "Bank Settlement with Kennedy, Kidd & Co.", S&P Jarvis Papers, loc. cit.

(15) As to the Bank's opening date, see J.S. Baldwin to J. Quesnel, March 22, 1827. *Quesnel Papers*, loc. cit.

(16) Peter MacArthur, Footnote "13" above.

of York," wrote one contemporary observer, "is a large handsome building, entered by a flight of stone steps; having doors, and the fittings up in the inside, of mahogany."(17)

The Bank of Upper Canada's move to the corner of Duke and George Streets was followed by unparalleled growth in York and the surrounding country, as well as for the bank. "Look at York -how it flourishes. All is owing to their having a bank", noted the *Canadian Freeman* of February 17, 1831.

In part, the bank's flourishing was due to the fact that it was the only bank and the financial agent of the government of the Province during a wildcat economic boom. Between 1830 and 1834 when York's name was changed to Toronto and it was incorporated as a city, the population increased from 2,860 to 9,252 — in spite of fatal cholera epidemics in 1832 and 1834.(18) Building lots were no longer to be found in the town, and the price of land multiplied.

The Bank flourishes — early management

In part as well, the bank's flourishing was due to its management. Its president from the time of its incorporation until 1835 was William Allan (1770-1853). Allan was a Scot who had come to Niagara in 1788 and to York in 1797. His obvious abilities had made him York's leading merchant from the time of the War of 1812 until he sold his store in 1822. While he avoided direct participation in elected politics he was no stranger to office.(19) The bank's first cashier or general manager, Thomas Gibbs Ridout (1792-1861), served from May 1822 until April 1861. Son of Surveyor-General Thomas Ridout, Thomas Gibbs Ridout was trained as a civil servant, handling large sums of money as purchasing agent with the Commissariat Department during the War of 1812, a position which lasted until 1820. Although he was a moderate in politics and economics, Ridout was accepted by the bank's more conservative directors as York had few other well-trained executives to choose from. As one of the bank's directors put it,"for

Matilda Ann Ridout, 1847   **Thomas Gibbs Ridout, 1847**
Watercolours by Hoppner Meyer
Courtesy Metropolitan Toronto Library Board

Hoppner Meyer, an artist who resided in Toronto from 1841, had, according to the *British Colonist* of Sept. 10, 1847, recently completed portraits "of Thomas G. Ridout, Esq., and lady, in which it is not too much to say, he has been eminently successful. That of Mr. Ridout is what is generally described as 'a striking likeness' which indeed it is." The authors are indebted for this reference to Mary Allodi of the Canadiana Section, Royal Ontario Museum, as well as to John Ridout.

application, correctness and attention to business you will clearly not find his equal".(20) Ridout and his family lived on the second floor of the Bank of Upper Canada building from the time of its opening in 1827, until 1861.

(17) Quoting George Henry (1831). See Firth, the *op. cit.*, Vol. 2 p.331.

(18) Firth, *op. cit.* Vol. 2 p. lxxxii.

(19) See: "William Allan a Pioneer Business Executive", unpublished manuscript by Maxwell A. Magill, *Magill Papers*, Queens University Archives. See also: "Founders of Canadian Banking, the Hon. Wm. Allan Merchant and Banker", by Adam Shortt, *Journal of the Canadian Bankers Association* Vol. xxx (1923) pp. 154-156.
See also: Firth *op. cit.* Vol. II pp 50-51, Allan served as York's postmaster from 1808 [*York Gazette*, Aug. 29,1807, Jan. 27, 1808, Jan. 4, 1809] to 1828, Collector of Customs, Inspector of

Licenses, Treasurer of the District, Justice of the Peace, Colonel of the 3rd Regiment York Militia, Commissioner of the Canada Company after 1829, Member of the Legislative Council, 1825, the Executive Council from 1836, and first Governo r of the British American Fire & Life Assurance Co. from 1836.

(20) John S. Baldwin to Julius Quesnel, January 10, 1833, S. 85 Vol. 1 No. 45. *J.R. McMurrich Collection*, Baldwin Room Metropolitan Toronto Library. See also article by Robert J. Burns on "Thomas Gibbs Ridout," *Dictionary of Canadian Biography*. Vol. IX (University of Toronto Press, Toronto, 1976). pp.661-663.

Allan was bolstered by a majority of directors who supported the bank's policy of "soft" money, allowing the bank to be used as an instrument of government policy in making large loans, which while lucrative were not necessarily based on ordinary banking principles. Three times, between 1825 and 1835, the "soft" money group led by the Boultons, the Robinsons and the Anglican archdeacon John Strachan beat back electoral challenges by the "hard" money group led by the Ridout and Baldwin families.(21)

While William Allan had not taken sides in the 1825 election, by 1830 he felt that the Baldwins and Ridouts were organizing to prevent him from being elected as president again.(22) Allan jumped into the battle and obtained enough proxies from absent shareholders to ensure his re-election and that of "the Court Party" at the annual meeting on June 7th. But tempers were high, and to make matters worse, William Lyon Mackenzie, the radical editor of the *Colonial Advocate*, appeared at the meeting at the bank's head office with a number of proxies and participated loudly. The *York Courier* reported that Mackenzie was "lance corporal" of a "political squad" that failed to get their "associates" on the board.(23) For T.G. Ridout, the Cashier, the election was a near disaster. William Allan confided to an associate that "I am told our Cashier is at the bottom of all or the prime mover of all that was attempted. I am sorry for it but I fear it to be true. He is very ungrateful but that is nothing new. He has an ungovernable temper".(24)

Allan's concern over the cashier's ambitions put the relationship under considerable stress, aggravated from Ridout's side by a succession of personal tragedies.(25) In the end, it was undoubtedly Ridout's

irreplaceable ability to administer a sophisticated financial institution that kept him in his position.

By 1835 Allan, disgusted with the unrewarding nature of his work, decided to retire. He was replaced as president by William Proudfoot, who, Allan felt, "was not elected from the idea of being either equal to it or the best they could get. He was the only one who was a candidate for it".(26) Proudfoot's biographer felt that "it was his inoffensiveness, almost to the point of nonentity" which partly explains his survival in office till 1861. During Proudfoot's long tenure as the bank's president, Ridout, as cashier, had far more real and acknowledged influence than his president.(27)

---

(21) See "John Baldwin: Portrait of a Colonial Entrepreneur" by T.W. Acheson, *Ontario History*, Vol. 61. (1969) pp.153-166.

(22) William Allan to John Macaulay, April 12, 1830. *John Macaulay Papers*, Public Archives of Ontario.

(23) As reprinted in the *Kingston Chronicle*, June 19, 1830.

(24) William Allan to John Macaulay, June 19, 1830, *Macaulay Papers* loc. cit. The letter continued: "Him and his brother Frank in the Bank have been quarrelling for the last six months & complain to me. He and all the rest get on very well."

(25) Ridout's father, who had been surety for his conduct as cashier, had died in 1829. In August, 1830, Ridout's brother Frank, his employee at the Bank, was found to have stolen £1,600 and in October he was sentenced to nine months in prison. Ridout, mortified, made good the loss personally, rather than call on his brother's sureties, one of whom was Archdeacon Strachan (Strachan to Macaulay, August 16, 1828). Strachan was "sorry, for the wretched young man & his family from this disposition and other bereavements were already very miserable". By October, the Bank's board insisted that Ridout provide five new sureties satisfactory to them to guarantee his own conduct. At least one of Ridout's nominees failed to be approved by the Bank's board. Finally, John S. Baldwin reluctantly agreed to fill the last position as Ridout's surety because "a man ought not to be left destitute" (Baldwin to Quesnel, November 1, 1830, *J.R. McMurrich*

Collection, loc. cit. Vol. I, No. 39A) In January, 1832, Ridout's wife, Louisa, died of cholera as well. John Baldwin commented that Ridout was "very much inclined to allow himself to sink under the feelings of reflecting too frequently on his late losses...unless (he) recovers from his present state may lose his place". (J.S. Baldwin to Julius Quesnel, January 10, 1832. *J.R. McMurrich Collection*, loc. cit. Vol. I, No. 45.

(26) William Allan to John Macaulay, June 9, 1835. *Macaulay Papers*, loc. cit. In 1834, when Allan had indicated an intention to retire from the presidency of the Bank of Upper Canada, John Baldwin was promoted by the moderates as a possible candidate to succeed him. Allan, while acknowledging that Baldwin was the ablest possible replacement, was prevailed upon by "the government party" to remain in office as there was "a good deal of bad feeling against that *Family &* connection". Baldwin was not re-elected as a Director in the 1834 elections and later confided to his friend in Montreal that he "perhaps never will run again...I consider myself ill-used in the Bank election owing to the Scandalous and Shameful way tis managed (that is the Elections)". (Baldwin to Quesnel, May 22, 1837, *J.R. McMurrich Collection*. loc. cit. Vol. II, 126.

(27) Barrie Dyster's article on "William Proudfoot" in the *Dictionary of Canadian Biography*. Vol. IX (University of Toronto Press, Toronto, 1976) pp. 647-648. The biography does not supply birth or death dates because Proudfoot "left so little impress on the minds and memories of his contemporaries that his death apprently passed as unnoticed as his birth".

134

BANK OF UPPER CANADA.

CHARTERED BY ACT OF PARLIAMENT.

GOVERNMENT DIRECTORS.

The Hon. G. H. Markland.	The Hon. Joseph Wells.
" John H. Dunn.	Christopher Widmer Esqr.

DIRECTORS CHOSEN BY THE STOCKHOLDERS.

The Hon. William Allan, President

J. S. Baldwin Esqr.	Alexander Wood Esqr.
Wm. Gamble Esqr.	Robert Gillespie Esqr.
Wm. Proudfoot Esqr.	David Stegman Esqr.
Benjn. Thorn Esqr.	D'Arcy Boulton Esqr.
J. P. Jarvis Esqr.	Wm. H. Draper Esqr.

Thomas Gibbs Ridout Esqr., Cashier.
Robert Horne Esqr. Teller.
Mr. Charles S. Murray, Book-keeper.
  " John Mosley, Assistant do.
  " Edward Goldsmith. do. do.
  " Robert G. Anderson, Second Teller.
  " Richard Richardson Discount Clerk
  " Maurice Scollard, Clerk
  " Joseph S. Lee, do
  " William Hamilton, do.
  " John Maitland, Messenger.

Office at Kingston, John Macaulay Esqr., Cashier.
  " Cobourg, James G. Bethune Esqr. do.
  " Brockville, Joseph Wenham Esqr. do.
  " Niagara, Thomas McCormack Esq. do.
  " Hamilton, Andrew Stephen Esqr do.
Agent at Prescott, Alpheus Jones Esqr.
  " Amherstburg, Hon. Jas. Gordon.
  " Bytown, G. W. Baker Esqr.
  " Penetanguishine, And. Mitchell Esqr
  " London, England, Thomas Wilson and Co.
  " New-York, Prime, Ward, King and Co.
  " Montreal, Montreal Bank.

NOTE.—Discount day Wednesday of every week : notes offered for discount, must be put under cover to the Cashier, and left at the Bank the day before.

A page from the *York Commercial Directory, 1833-34*

William Allan, c.1850
First President of the Bank of Upper Canada
1821-1835
Courtesy Metropolitan Toronto Library Board

Moving towards Rebellion

The greatest physical challenge to the bank came at the beginning of Proudfoot's term. The position of the Family Compact and its control of the government had come increasingly under attack by those who were excluded from it. While the Reformers had a majority in the elected Assembly of the Province, the power of government was exercised through an appointed Legislative Council, which could veto the Assembly's statutes or replace its decisions with its own legislation. More important, all political power was exercised by an Executive Council or cabinet appointed to advise the Lieutenant-Governor. In 1836, the new Lieutenant-Governor, Sir Francis Bond Head, used the authority of his office to defeat the Reformers in the elections and to return a "loyal" House of Assembly.(28) From that date the moderate Reformers withdrew from active politics, leaving the Radical faction exposed as the only opposition. The Radicals, led by William Lyon Mackenzie and those still outspoken enough to criticize the government, found themselves more and more in the position of being "disloyal". Aggravated by a severe economic depression, the few remaining commercial opportunities were, in the view of the Radicals, exploited by the ruling group and "their" bank.

In 1837, word of the failure of some banks in the United States was spreading northward, putting fear in the hearts, not only of the depositors of the Bank of Upper Canada, but also of those who held its notes and obligations. By May, the fear was turning to panic, a state that Mackenzie did his best to foster through the columns of his new newspaper, *The Constitution.*

An Election in Upper Canada during the 1830s
C.W. Jeffreys. Courtesy Public Archives of Canada

"Bank Vengeance: We learned from good authority that the President, directors and Co. of the B.U.C. have dismissed from his situation, Mr. John Maitland the Bank Messenger, for the crime of freely exercising his privilege in voting for an independent candidate at the last election"

The Advocate, April 3, 1834

---

(28) By all accounts, Head, when he was appointed Lieutenant Governor at the end of 1835, had no previous relevant experience in business, war or politics and had never been to North America. By some accounts he was mistakenly appointed in place of his cousin, Sir Edmund Head, Governor General of Canada in the 1850s, or his brother, Sir George Head, a senior military officer who had written a book about his five years experience in North America. See: William Kilbourn, *The Firebrand*, (Toronto, Clarke Irwin & Company, Ltd. 1956), pp. 128-129.

William Lyon Mackenzie
(1795 — 1861)
c.1855

Sir Francis Bond Head
(1817-1892), *Lieutenant-
Governor of Upper Canada, 1837*

*Courtesy Metropolitan Toronto
Library Board*

A run on the bank began on May 19th, 1837. John S. Baldwin, a former director, was there and gave this account:

> the Bank of a sudden became full of people demanding *cash cash* for notes and up to this hour 2 o'clock Monday tis with the greatest difficulty a person can get to the counter to transact any little matter they may want the hugh [sic] and cry is up on all quarters amongst the ignorant that the Bank is gon [sic], the Bank is gon, and all Such Stuff it has extended to Markham, Whitechurch, Toronto and in fact all the Back Settlements, So that they the people are seen coming in waggons freely to town to get their notes redeemed frightened that they may lose them. There is one very peculiar feature in the description of the applicants within the last three days, that is they consist of a dirty vagabond looking Set, Such as Carters, labourers about buildings and idlers, all of the city with a few farmers mixed among them now the first description of

persons could not have the means of keeping up such a run So that I feel confident they are agents of Scoundrels in the City who are ashamed to be seen acting personally and adopt there [sic] means to accomplish their design.(29)

The bank survived the panic for four weeks, largely through the aid of an additional loan from the government. The directors were no doubt also assisted by a number of their friends who lined the counter asking for coin in return for their own notes. According to Robertson's *Landmarks of Toronto* "what was paid out to them during the day was trundled back in a wheelbarrow at night". On June 19th, the Legislative authorized the bank to suspend specie payments and the crisis subsided.

When armed rebellion actually broke out in December, 1837, the Bank of Upper Canada was again at the centre of the conflict. It was the object of the Rebels as they marched down Yonge Street on the afternoon of December 5th, only to be stopped by a small force of Loyalists who ambushed them near College Street. Two days later, even as the Rebels were being routed by Loyalist forces at Montgomery's Tavern (near Eglinton Avenue), they dispatched a second force of about 50 men to again attack the bank — this time from the east across the bridge over the Don River.

John S. Baldwin, who considered himself "a free agent to speak about what I hear in the Street", wrote his own account of the events of the week to his former partner in Montreal:

> On Tuesday morning [December 5th]about 1 o'clock our City and Church bells rung the Alarm, and the word was that rebel forces under Mackenzie, Gibson and others were within 5 miles of town ...[T]he word was that there [sic] great object was the Bank which they intended to rob & in which there is little short of £140,000 in Gold & Silver, this was soon well guarded, as were all the adjoining houses, so that those who were judges said 1,000 men could not take it.

(29) J.S. Baldwin to Julius Quesnel, May 22, 1837, *J.R. McMurrich Collection* loc. cit. Vol. II, No. 126.

The Bank Guard

From the first hours of the Rebellion the security of the Bank of Upper Canada was recognized as paramount. An eyewitness account stated that on December 5th "a strong garrison was thrown into the Bank of Upper Canada, which, being a stone building is capable of repelling the assaults of any foe not supported by Artillery".(32)

While the most serious clashes of the Rebellion in Upper Canada fasted for only three days, threats of attacks from rebel sympathizers, and even the occasional skirmish, lasted throughout the next year. The "Bank Guard" was formed on December 5th, 1837 and disbanded by January 27, 1839. Composed of a uniformed force of 36 of the elite of the community with T.G. Ridout as its captain, the Guard was on duty in the bank for the entire time up to April 30, 1838, and again after October 27, 1838.(See Appendix II) A description of the Guard survives in the form of a letter from one of its junior officers, W.W. Street, a teller in the bank:

My dearest Mother, I should have answered your letter long before this but have so many engagements in the shape of Guard every night at the Bank and drills daily besides my Bank duty and writing to England, that my days are fully occupied — we have here a regularly organized Guard of 1 Capt 2 Lieuts 2 Sergts 2 Corpls and 29 Rank & file all respectable fellows — We throw our pay and rations into a mess fund which is thus very respectably kept up — one third of our numbers is on guard nightly and as we are frequently turned out for the different visiting rounds and patrols we have little or no sleep, not being allowed to take off our Clothes or accoutrements — It is rather hard duty and will probably last at least all the winter — We keep up our Barricades and have 2 Cannonades — 9 pounders. There are 4 Companies of City Guards mustering about 200 men — The Board of Directors voted the Bank Guard £200 for uniforms, which are now being made — They are very neat and gentlemanly — A Blue fine Cloth frock coat with stand up Collar, on which as well as on the Cuffs is some black Velvet and braid — black silk buttons — Oil skin military Cap and trousers of fine dark cloth with a red cord down the seam....(33)

Marching down Yonge Street

C.W. Jeffreys. Courtesy Public Archives of Canada

"The word was that their great object was the Bank . . ."

J.S. Baldwin, December 1837

The attack was renewed two days later:

[A]bout 50 of the rebels were dispatched from the main body that very morning [Thursday] and sent to the eastward, crossed the Don about 5 miles up and came down in the Eastern side, as soon as they reached the Kingston road these scoundrels began to plunder and burn, they destroyed a large new building intended for a Brewery, also a tavern and one or two small dwellings from what I here [sic] they were intended as a devotion [sic] in favour of the main body who were determined if they did anything to attack the Bank — but I trust that quiet is secured for some time to come.(30)

Similarly *The Patriot*, the unofficial voice of the Family Compact, carried a news report on December 5th, 1837, that the rebels "were certainly determined last night to pounce upon the Bank, the arms at City Hall, and the ammunition at the Garrison". A week later *The Patriot* noted that Mackenzie had escaped to Buffalo, N.Y. and was trying to raise a force sympathetic to the Rebellion "promising them LANDS AND THE PLUNDER OF THE BANK OF UPPER CANADA, *which*, said he '*was never known to have so much money in it before*'."(31)

(30) J.S. Baldwin to Julius Quesnel, December 8, 1837, (typescript), *Quesnel Papers*, AAN. See also, Baldwin to Quesnel, May 22, 1837 *supra*.

(31) *The Patriot*, (Toronto), December 5, 1837 and December 15, 1837. Microfilm, PAO.

(32) *ibid.* December 15, 1837 EXTRA

(33) W.W. Street to his mother, January 17, 1838. Copy in *Max Magill Papers*, loc. cit. See also the enlightening paper on "The Social Composition of the Toronto Bank Guards, 1837-38" by J.K. Johnston, *Ontario History*, Vol. 64 (1972) pp. 95-104. Street started as private but was promoted to corporal on March 31, 1838.

The bank building was so well fortified that it was used during this period as a place of safe-keeping for the city's mail,(34) as the repository of the province's gold (until it was transferred to the newly constructed garrison at Fort York in November 1838)(35) and finally as the temporary residence and place of refuge for Robert B. Sullivan, the Chairman of the Executive Council (or "Premier of the Council of Ministers") of the Province.(36) The Bank Guard spent much of its time in Ridout's private quarters on the second floor of the bank building.(37) John A. Macdonald, then a young law student, had "pleasant recollections of dining with the Bank Guard over the old Upper Canada Bank", after his tour of duty with the Loyalist force at Montgomery's Tavern.(38)

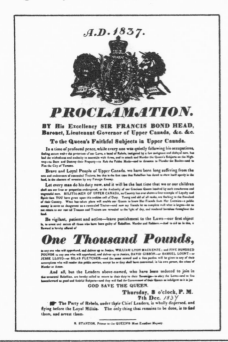

(34) James S. Howard to the Earl of Lichfield, Postmaster General, March 16, 1838. Published in *A Statement of Facts Relative to the Dismissal of James S. Howard, Esq. Late Postmaster of the City of Toronto, U.C.* (The Guardian, 1839), page 11.

(35) T.G. Ridout to Matilda Ridout, November 12, 1838. *Thomas Gibbs Ridout Papers*, PAO.

(36) *ibid.*, November 22, 1838.

(37) T.G. Ridout to Matilda Ridout, January 27, 1839, *Ridout Papers*, loc. cit. "I have got entirely rid of the Bank Guard and consequently more comfortable. Miss Davis has made new brown Holland covers for the arm chair and sopha - which saves your blue moreens.* The old ones were entirely worn out and looked precious shabby..."

(*moreen: a strong fabric of wool, wool and cotton, or cotton with a plain glossy or moiré finish)

(38) Sir John A. Macdonald to Sir James Gowan, December 13, 1887, published in *Ontario History*, Volume 60 (1968) pp. 62-63.

The Bank Guard, *stationed at the Bank of Upper Canada building to guard the Bank and Post Office, December 1837 to January 1839*
Watercolour by Julian Mulock

John George Howard
1803-1890

Architect for alterations to the Bank of Upper Canada Building. 1843-1846

The 1840s

The 1840s were a decade of quiet growth for the Bank of Upper Canada. After the Rebellion and as a result of Lord Durham's investigation and report, the provinces of Upper and Lower Canada were merged, in 1841, into a new Province of Canada with its capital in Montreal. For the Bank of Upper Canada this meant that its official position as government fiscal agent passed to the Bank of Montreal, and the government of the province ended its official connection by selling its Bank shares.

At the same time, Thomas G. Ridout and his "hard money" group emerged as being in undisputed control of the bank and it continued to prosper. There was one attempt to turn out Proudfoot and "old Tom" in this period. In June, 1848, a group headed by Samuel Jarvis, the Boultons, and William Cayley attempted to replace Proudfoot and Ridout with Allan MacNab and William Cayley as president and cashier respectively. In the resulting elections, Cayley, Jarvis and most of their supporters lost their seats on the Board of Directors.(39)

In 1843 the bank's Board of Directors had decided to make alterations to the bank, not only to reinforce its image of importance but also to increase its security. For the contemplated work, Ridout engaged John G. Howard, undoubtedly the city's most eminent ar-

chitect of that decade. Howard (1803-1890) had been born near London, England, and had come to York in 1832. He designed a number of important buildings in Toronto including the third jail, the lunatic asylum on Queen Street East, the 6th Post Office, the Bank of British North America, the House of Industry and many others. He gave High Park and his house, Colbourne Lodge, to the city upon his death.(40)

Howard designed and supervised the construction of the bank's stone porch in 1843. That same year he had iron columns cast in Niagara to his designs — the same iron columns which still grace the former main banking room on the ground floor. At the same time he likely added the enormous iron-studded security doors, which fit neatly against the pilasters surrounding the inside of the main entrace doors when not in use. In 1846, he added the wrought iron railing around the top of the portico.(41)

The Beginning of the End

The burning of the Parliament Buildings in Montreal in 1849 by a mob demanding the Governor-General sign the "Rebellion Losses" Bill was an event that started the Bank of Upper Canada into its greatest expansion and sowed the seeds for its ultimate collapse seventeen years later.

A year after the Parliament Buildings were burned, the Government of the Province of Canada (which covered what is now the provinces of Ontario and Quebec) moved the provincial capital from Montreal to Toronto, at the same time changing its official bank from the Bank of Montreal to the Bank of Upper Canada.

In order to accommodate the increased government business, the Bank of Upper Canada entered a program of expansion, coinciding with a speculative boom in the economy. To provide more space for its staff, the cashier, T.G. Ridout, moved his family from the second floor of the bank building at Duke and George Streets to a new residential addition that was constructed immediately to the north of the bank in 1851. Additional branches, designed by Frederick Cumberland, architect, were constructed in bustling cities and towns such as Windsor, Sarnia, Port Hope and Quebec. As the province's

(39) See: L. Heyden to Robert Baldwin May 22, 1848, *Robert Baldwin Papers*, MTPL A50:99; Larratt Smith to his father June 29, 1849 *Larratt Smith Letters*, MTPL.

(40) Firth, *op.cit.,* Volume II, p.83.

(41) Baldwin Room MTPL, *John G. Howard Papers*, daybooks 1843: January 23, 24; February 11-14; August 2, 7, 11, 25, 28; October 4, 5, 6, 7; November 24, 27. 1846: May 18. For these references I am indebted to Shirley Moriss and Stephen Otto.

FRONT·ELEVATION·OF·PORCH

BANK·OF·UPPER·CANADA

·SHOWING·POSITION·OF·RAILING·

Scale   0   2   4   6   8   10   Feet.

Measured drawing of the portico of the Bank of Upper Canada Building
by Donald J. Reed under the supervision of Professor Eric Arthur, 1931
Courtesy Public Archives of Ontario

official bank, the Bank of Upper Canada was given the right to mint coinage and in fact, penny and half-penny "St. George Tokens" were issued in 1850, 1852, 1854 and 1857. (42) At the same time the bank took on the accounts of the Great Western Railway as well as of the Grand Trunk Railway, which was inaugurating the period of railway construction in Canada by its initial line from Toronto to Quebec.

The bank's government business proved a threat as well as an opportunity. In the 1820s, Ridout and the "hard money" faction had opposed unsound banking practices motivated by the bank's role as official financial agent. Now in the 1850s, the "hard money" concept

was once again losing control of the bank's administration because of the bank's close link with the government.

The commercial crisis of 1857-1858, coinciding with two bad harvests, severely tested the stability of the bank and brought its intrinsic "soft money" vulnerability as an agent of the government to the fore. In March, 1857, when a passenger train broke through the

---

(42) The Province of Canada issued its own coinage based on the decimal system in 1858.

"Scene of the fearful railroad accident at the bridge over the Desjardin Canal, Canada."

Courtesy Metropolitan Toronto Library Board

bridge at the Desjardin Canal near Hamilton, one of the 59 dead was Samuel Zimmerman, the most famous Canadian railway contractor of the day.(43) Zimmerman's railway ventures had been partly funded by the Zimmerman Bank, of which 98.2% of the shares were owned by Samuel Zimmerman personally. At the time of his death, Zimmerman's Bank was heavily indebted to the Government of the Province of Canada. Later that year, by a process which had no business justification, the Government instructed the Bank of Upper Canada to assume the government's debt from the Zimmerman Bank. This amounted to almost £250,000 — in addition to Zimmerman's personal debt of £325,000 which the Bank of Upper Canada already held.(44)

The Grand Trunk Railway, a venture sponsored jointly by the Canadian government and private enterprise, was the other major source of debt for the bank. Large sums were advanced by the bank to the Grand Trunk in circumstances that made it unclear whether the loans were guaranteed by the Government.(45) By 1859, the uncollectable debts from Zimmerman amounted to £580,000 and from the Grand Trunk, £415,000. An additional doubtful debt from the Great West Railway was £560,000.(46) In that year, William Cayley, who had been unsuccessful in the attempt to become cashier in 1848, was installed as the Government's nominee as assistant manager of the

bank. Calling the Zimmerman debt the "great incubus", Cayley concluded that "the Bank has also been led to make advances arising out of its connection with the Government and its desire to maintain the credit of the Banking Institutions of the Province which have proved a heavy burden".(47)

By the beginning of 1860, the blame for the bank's troubles was being assessed. One correspondent heard that the directors were contemplating "the dismissal of both the old men who have been at the head of the concern for some years" — Messrs. Proudfoot and Ridout, the president and cashier.(48) In March of the following year, Proudfoot and Ridout agreed to resign in favour of William Cayley, as the new president, and Robert Cassels as the new cashier. As a con-

(43) See "One Bold Operator: Samuel Zimmerman Niagara Entrepreneur, 1843-1857" by J.K. Johnston, *Ontario History*, Vol. 74 (1982) pp.26-44.

(44) *ibid*. p. 39. See also: T.G. Ridout to G.C. Glyn. April 30, 1859, *Glyn Mills & Co. Papers*, FA 272 PAC.

(45) See unpublished essay "Glyn's and Canada" page 11, *Glyn Mills & Co. Papers*, loc. cit.

(46) T.G. Ridout to Blackwell, April 16, 1859. T.G. Ridout to G.C. Glyn April 16, 1859. *Glyn Mills & Co. Papers*, loc. cit.

(47) William Cayley to G.C. Glyn, June 8, 1859. *Glyn Mills & Co. Papers*, loc. cit.

(48) D.L. MacPherson to A.T. Galt, January 3, 1860. *Galt Papers*, MG27-ID8 PAC.

dition for the resignations and new appointments, the Government had promised financial aid to the bank.(49)

Ridout was formally replaced in April, 1861, his salary continued to July 1, 1861. At the annual meeting at the end of June, Proudfoot, Cayley and Ridout all ran for the Board of Directors. Proudfoot and Cayley were not elected; Ridout received no votes.(50)

Thomas Gibbs Ridout died on July 29, 1861 — by a "singular coincidence" on the very same day the bank opened its new head office at Yonge and Colbourne Streets, and closed its office at Duke and George Streets.(51)

The bank continued to keep the official business of the Province until January 1, 1864, when it was transferred to the Bank of Montreal. On September 18, 1866, the Bank of Upper Canada closed its doors and went into receivership.

Another chapter in the story of the buildings at Duke and George had ended.

---

(49) William Proudfoot to G.C. Glyn, March 25, 1861. Cayley to Glyn, March 28, 1861. Cayley to Glyn, April 11, 1861. *Glyn Mills & Co. Papers*, loc. cit.

(50) Cassels to Glyn, 27 June, 1861, *Glyn Mills & Co. Papers*, loc. cit.

(51) See Article "Thomas Gibbs Ridout" *Sketches of Celebrated Canadians*, Henry James Morgan, (Hunter Rose & Co., Quebec, 1862), p.730-732.

Photograph of the Bank of Upper Canada head office, c.1859
Armstrong Beere and Hime, Toronto
Courtesy Metropolitan Toronto Library Board

THE 1851 ADDITION ON GEORGE STREET

As official agent of the Province of Canada, the Bank of Upper Canada had outgrown its headquarters by 1850 and, according to the City Directory of that year, it was understood "that it is in contemplation to enlarge the buildings at an early period".(1)

At the same time, Thomas G. Ridout's family, living on the second floor of the bank building and using the basement as a kitchen, had run out of space. After the death of his first wife, Ridout had remarried. He married his second wife, Matilda Ann, daughter of the English merchant Thomas Bramley, on September 6, 1834. In addition to Ridout's surviving son by his first marriage, Thomas and Matilda Ridout had eight children by 1850.(2)

The Bank of Upper Canada engaged the firm of Cumberland & Ridout to design a residential addition along George Street to the north of the bank to house the Ridout family and to allow the bank room to expand to the second floor of the main building.

Cumberland & Ridout was a partnership of Frederick William Cumberland (1821-1881) and Thomas Ridout, Junior, that lasted from January 1, 1850 until 1852.(3) Cumberland, the senior partner, had come to Toronto in 1847 after studying architecture in England with Sir Charles Barry while he was working on the Houses of Parliament at Westminster. He was "a great architect" according to one authority, who left an unequalled impression on his time.(4) He was, according to another, "the major builder and architect of the period".(5) He was responsible for the construction of St. James Cathedral in 1850, the Normal School building on Gould Street (later part of Ryerson Institute) in 1852, the Adelaide Court House on Adelaide Street East in the same year, the Seventh Post Office on Toronto Street in 1853, University College in 1856 and alterations to Osgoode Hall in 1857.(6)

Thomas Ridout, Junior, was born in 1828 in the Bank of Upper Canada building and was the only surviving child of Thomas G. Ridout's first marriage to Louisa Sullivan. Trained in engineering rather than architecture, he took a position as assistant engineer with the Great Western Railway in 1853 after leaving Cumberland's office.(7)

Cumberland had a close connection with Thomas G. Ridout not only because of his partnership with his son. He had married Wilmot Bramley, sister to Matilda Ridout, and lived at the north-west corner of Duke and George Streets, just across the street from the Ridouts, during the 1850s.(8) After 1852, in partnership with W.G. Storm, Cumberland prepared plans for several branches of the bank in other cities and towns.(9)

The addition on George Street was finished in 1851.(10) It was a three-storey building of yellow brick in the Flemish bond pattern common at the time. It had two chimneys at the north end, and a central chimney in the peak of the roof. It was joined to the Bank of Upper Canada building on the second floor by a wide panelled staircase.

Thomas G. Ridout made a number of changes to the surrounding grounds as well. "I have made some improvements outside of the house and in the garden since you left," Ridout wrote to his wife in 1853 after she had gone to visit her family in England. "The pump yard and the small north yard are well gravelled and so on to the street gate; a patch 9 feet wide is made of gravel — the garden walls are also gravelled and my melons and cucumbers are looking very well. So is the big grapevine — the onion patch is weeded."(11)

Even in the 1850s it was common for houses in town to keep barnyard animals. "The three ducks are out with 25 young ones" Ridout wrote to his wife. "I have put them all under the sweet plum tree and they are doing very well. The ponies and Jerry [the horse] are enjoying themselves in their pasture — and the cows supply us with more

(1) *Rowsell's City of Toronto & County of York Directory*, 1850-51, J. Armstrong, Editor (Henry Rowsell, Toronto, 1850) corrected to 1 January, 1850, page xxxiii.

(2) *Ridout Papers*, PAO, MV2393 envelope 44. See also the article on "Thomas Gibbs Ridout" by Robert J. Burns in the *Dictionary of Canadian Biography* Vol. IX (University of Toronto Press, Toronto, 1976) pp.661-663.

(3) Notice of partnership was published in the *British Colonist* (Toronto) March 8, 1850 page 4 and in the *Examiner* (Toronto), March 20, 1850 page 1. Cumberland and Ridout, Junior, continued in their business relationship throughout the 1850s, though on a less formal basis; *T.G. Ridout Papers*, Public Archives of Ontario, T.G. Ridout to Matilda Ridout, August 19, 1855.

(4) *Toronto No Mean City*, Eric Arthur (University of Toronto Press, 1964, 2nd Edition 1974) Appendix A, Page 245.

(5) *Toronto - Romance of a Great City*, by Katherine Hale (Cassell & Company Ltd. Toronto, 1956) page 113.

(6) Arthur, *op. cit.* p.245.

(7) Burns, *op. cit.* p.661.

(8) *Ridout Papers*, loc. cit. Note: (undated) "Grandma Bramley's Daughters, Matilda Ridout and Wilmot Cumberland".

(9) Plans for the Windsor (1855) and Sarnia (1855-57) branches are on file in the *Horwood Collection*, PAO.

(10) According to the 1852 City of Toronto assessment records, the value of the buildings on the lot owned by the Bank of Upper Canada was increased by 25% in that year. See *City of Toronto Assessment Records, 1847-1857*, City of Toronto Archives.

(11) Thomas G. Ridout to Matilda Ridout, June 6, 1853, *ibid.*

(12) Thomas G. Ridout to Matilda Ridout, June 21, 1853, *ibid.*

Matilda Bramley Ridout, c.1860
Photograph
Courtesy Public Archives of Ontario

Thomas Gibbs Ridout, c.1860
Cashier of the Bank of Upper
Canada, 1822-1861

Watercolour
Courtesy Metropolitan Toronto Library Board

butter and milk than we want. The Sisters of Charity get a large kettle of milk every day — we have bought no butter since you left us — not withstanding that buttered toast reigns paramount in kitchen and parlour, morning and evening."(12)

The Ridouts had three more children during the 1850s; a total of five daughters and six sons in addition to Thomas, Junior.

By 1857, at the age of 65, Ridout was at the peak of his career. In 1853 his salary as cashier has been raised from £750 to £1,000.(13) It was at this time that he contacted his brother-in-law, Frederick Cumberland, and had him do plans for a grand home at the head of Sherbourne Street, on land his family had bought in 1818. The foundations of the house, to be known as Sherborne Villa, were laid in 1857.(14) Cumberland designed a grand entrance hall with the same tiled floor, imported from England, as he had specified for the entrance halls of University College and Osgoode Hall.

By April, 1861 when Ridout was dismissed as cashier of the Bank of Upper Canada with his salary to terminate on July 1st, the house was not finished. Ridout sold it at the end of June at a devastating loss.

One month later on July 29, 1861, Ridout died. The family still lived in the building on George Street.(15)

A few months later, after the Ridout's had left the house, it was rented to J.W.G. Whitney who lived there with his family until the Bank failed in 1866.(16)

West side of the Bank of Upper Canada building showing 1851 addition, c. 1900

Courtesy Ontario Archives, Hood Papers Picture Collection

Frederick William Cumberland
(1821—1881)

Architect for the addition to the
Bank of Upper Canada Building, 1850-1851

(13) Burns, *op. cit.*, p.663.

(14) Sherborne Villa was later called "Fudger House". It was demolished in 1964. *Toronto 100 Years of Grandeur* by Lucy Booth Martyn (Pagurian Press Limited, Toronto, 1978) pp. 128-132.

(15) Burns, *op. cit.*, p. 663.

(16) *Toronto City Directories*, 1862-1866.

Photograph c.1869 coloured with water colours to show the Fourth York Post Office, 1833-39
John Ross Robertson picture collection, The Baldwin Room
Courtesy The Metropolitan Toronto Board

THE POST OFFICE BUILDING

Salome MacLean Howard, c. 1835
Watercolour

Courtesy
Metropolitan Toronto Library Board

T he post office on Duke Street, in the Town of York, was opened in December, 1833, and remained in operation until the beginning of 1839. It was the fourth and last post office in York and the first post office in the City of Toronto. It was the scene of what must be the best documented drama of the 1837 Rebellion.

When James Scott Howard, Postmaster, moved the York Post Office to Duke Street near the Bank of Upper Canada in late December, 1833, the Town of York was in the midst of enormous changes. The population had more than tripled within the past five years (1), the government was considering incorporating the town as a city, and while it was not apparent to the inhabitants, the countryside was about to enter a period of economic depression and political upheaval.

Of course, York's growing pains were obvious to everyone. "Of all places I ever saw" observed one of the inhabitants, "this, the Capital of His Majesty's Province of U.C. is the most dirty. I do not know but a light bark canoe might sail through the muddy streets. An Act of Incorporation is talked of and then perhaps the lapse of a few years may make the Town tolerable for pedestrians."(2)

James Scott Howard was born in County Cork in Ireland in 1798. His grandfather, Nicola Huart or Houard, was a Huguenot who had left France after the revocation of the Edict of Nantes had ended toleration of Protestants. He had fled to Holland, reunited with his family in England and settled in Ireland where he changed his family name to Howard. His father, James Scott Howard, Senior, had converted to Methodism and James Scott Howard, Junior, himself, had been brought up in a strongly religious family. He emigrated from Cork in 1819 with Daniel Sullivan, and his family,(3) remaining in Fredericton, New Brunswick, for a time while the Sullivans went on to York.(4)

James Scott Howard, c. 1835
3rd York Postmaster, 1828-1834
1st City of Toronto Postmaster, 1834-1837
Watercolour

Courtesy
Metropolitan Toronto Library Board

---

(1) The population increased from 2,860 in 1830 to 9,252 by 2 June, 1834. See Edith Firth, *The Town of York 1815-1834, A further Collection of Documents of Early Toronto.* (The Champlain Society, University of Toronto Press, Toronto 1966) Vol. II, Introduction P.lxxxii.

(2) John Mann, York to Francis L. Walsh, Postmaster, Vittoria 10 December, 1833. Baldwin Room, Metropolitan Toronto Library.

(3) See *Firth, op. cit.,* pp.40-41 and 193n. Sullivan's wife, Barbara, was a sister to Dr. William Warren Baldwin of York, later to be architect of the Bank of Upper Canada Building on Duke Street. Among their eight children were - *Augusta Elizabeth,* who married her first cousin Robert

Baldwin in 1827, - *Louisa* who married Thomas Gibbs Ridout, the cashier of the Bank of Upper Canada, but died of cholera in 1832, - *Robert* (1802-1853) who became mayor of Toronto in 1835, and - *Augustus* (1814-1868). Both Robert and Augustus became lawyers and were members of the Legislative and Executive Councils of the Province of Upper Canada. See *ibid,* pp. 137 and 118. See also *Spadina, A Story of Old Toronto,* Austin Seton Thompson (Pagurian Press Limited, Toronto 1975). chart, p.xvi.

(4) *Howard (MacLean)Papers,* Public Archives of Ontario (PAO).

Upon his arrival in York in late 1819, he commenced working "as chief and only assistant to . . . William Allan in his respective offices of Postmaster, Collector of Customs, Inspector of licences and Treasurer of the District."(5) In 1822 he married Salome MacLean, the daughter of Archibald MacLean, who had served with the British during the American Revolution and had settled in Fredericton in 1783. They had two children, Prudence Eliza and Archibald MacLean, a third child having died in infancy.(6)

In July 1828 he was appointed York's third Postmaster, succeeding William Allan.(7) For his first year as Postmaster, Howard rented a log building on the south side of Duke Street between George and New (Jarvis) Streets as York's second Post Office. In 1829 he moved to a new office and residence on the west side of George Street between Duke and King Streets.(8)

Howard, staunchly religious, did not start with the trust of the majority he was to serve. "The Post Master here is a Methodist in whom I have no sort of confidence" wrote the Anglican Archdeacon John Strachan to a friend. "I am unwilling at times to shew [him] to who I correspond. This puts me sometimes to inconvenience."(9)

During the years of Howard's term as Postmaster, and indeed until 1851, the Postal Service was not administered by the province of Upper Canada but was a Department of the British Postal Service under the supervision of the Postmaster General and the Colonial Secretary in England. The resident head of the Postal Service in Canada was the Deputy Postmaster General for British North America, an official who was headquartered in Quebec City and was responsible only to his superiors in England. In his report of 1816, the Deputy Postmaster General had suggested that there should be a separate Deputy Postmaster General for Upper Canada as well as one for Lower Canada; and he had recommended William Allan, Postmaster of York for the position. The authorities in England had disapproved of the proposal, but in view of the advantages of having some official in

Upper Canada with wider authority than that of a mere postmaster, the position of York Postmaster became, from that date, the unofficial assistant Deputy Postmaster General for Upper Canada without any formal change in title.(10)

So it was that Howard, on his appointment, became the most important resident postal official in Upper Canada. His duties extended to supervision of other Post Offices in the area and finding candidates to serve in new offices as they were opened.(11)

The Deputy Postmaster-General during Howard's tenure as Postmaster was Thomas Allen Stayner (1788-1868). In 1827 Stayner had succeeded his father-in-law Daniel Sutherland in that position which he held until it was abolished in 1851. An efficient administrator, Stayner increased the number of post offices in his area from 80 in 1827 to 853 by 1851.(12)

Construction of the Fourth Post Office

In March, 1833, to keep pace with the enormous expansion of the population in York and the consequent increase of business, James Scott Howard set forth plans to construct a larger post office building. He entered into discussions with William Allan, then president of the Bank of Upper Canada, for the purchase of a lot near the bank at the corner of Duke and George Streets. The directors of the bank, seeing an opportunity for an expanded financial centre on their block within a year of losing their monopoly as the only chartered bank in Upper Canada, consented to sell the easterly 60 feet of their lot to its full depth of 200 feet. "But", wrote the bank's cashier to Howard, "this bargain is made with the full understanding and perfect confidence of your erecting a reputable brick building, such as the president stated he had seen a plan of at your house, and that it was your intention to erect; and also with the confidence that the Post Office establishment is to be kept in it."(13)

(5) Public Archives of Canada (PAC), G Series, Vol. 85, p.295 (J.S. Howard to The Earl of Lichfield, Postmaster General, February 22, 1838).
J.S. Howard to Thos. A. Stayner, Deputy Postmaster General, Quebec, January 29, 1829,"I am now nearly ten years in the P.O. ..." *Post Office Toronto Records*, 1828-1838, Baldwin Room, Metropolitan Toronto Library, Vol. 2.
William Allan (1770-1853) had a number of other offices. He also served as: Justice of the Peace, Acting Magistrate, Colonel of the 3rd Regiment, York Militia, First President of the Bank of Upper Canada 1822-1835, Commissioner of the Canada Company after 1829, 1st Governor of the British American Fire and Life Assurance Co. See *Firth*, Vol. II, pp.50-51.

(6) For biographical information see: Edward Marion Chadwick, *Ontarian Families*, 1894, pp.188-191 (reprinted by Hunterdon House, Lambertville, New Jersey, 1970); *Commemorative Biographical Record of the County of York, Ontario* (J.H. Beers & Co. Toronto, 1907) pp.277-278; *Macaulay Papers*, Public Archives of Ontario, James Scott Howard to John Macaulay, December 1, 1830.

(7) J.S. Howard to Thos. A. Stayner, Deputy Postmaster General, Quebec, July 12, 1828 "I have to acknowledge the receipt of your favour of the 4 Instant accompanied by my commission as Postmaster of this place...". *Post Office Toronto Records*, 1828-1838, Baldwin Room, Metropolitan Toronto Library, Vol. 2.

William Allan wrote officially recommending Howard's appointment: "I do not hesitate to say I think it very fortunate for the Dept your having a person to employ here so well acquainted with the duty and so faithful in all respects". William Allan to Daniel Sutherland, June 23, 1828, *William Allan Papers* "Account Book of the Post Office at York, 1824 to 1828", Metropolitan Toronto Public Library. Daniel Sutherland was Deputy Postmaster General until 1827 when he retired in favour of his son-in-law, Thomas Allen Stayner.

(8) Deed registered in City of Toronto Registry Office, August 15, 1829 as No. 6909.

(9) Strachan to John Macaulay, January 18, 1830, *Macaulay Papers*, PAO MS78.

(10) William Smith, *The History of the Post Office in British North America*, 1639-1870 (Cambridge University Press, 1920) p.104.

(11) Howard Letter Book, *Post Office Toronto Records*, loc. cit. Vol. 2.

(12) Andre Martineau "Thomas Allen Stayner" in the *Dictionary of Canadian Biography*. Vol. IX (University of Toronto Press, Toronto, 1976) pp.742-3.

(13) Letter from T.G. Ridout to James S. Howard, March 27, 1833, quoted in James S. Howard, *A Statement of Facts Relative to the Dismissal of James S. Howard, Esq. Late Postmaster of the City of Toronto, U.C.* (Toronto, J.H. Lawrence, printer, Guardian Office 1839) p.20.

James S. Howard Esq
To A. Hamilton Dr

June 24. 1833. To 1 Walnut Screw 2d — 1.0.0
26. Reglazing 3 panes e 5½ — 1.10½
Oct. 23. 3½ lbs White paint e 10 — 2.11
Dec. 17. To 204 panes 6×4 e 1 — 17.0
To numbering them 504 figures — 1.5.0
To Priming, Glazing & painting them 2 coats e 1d each — 1.10.7½
To painting 110 yds in Office e 4 — 5.10.—
do 83 ft Base in do e 2d — 13.10
Work done at Mr. Howards, Brother in laws — 17.9
Jan 24. 1834 Glazing 2 fanlights & 3½ to putty — 6.3
Reglazing 1 pane — 7
June 14 To 120 yds Sanded work e 1/3 — 7.10.0
To Painting, Graining & Varnishing Walnut 90 yds 1/6 — 6.15.0
do do do do 240 ft Base e 4 — 4.0.0
do do do do 40 ft String e 4 — 13.4
do do 33 yds Oak e 2 — 3.6.0
do do 35 ft Base e 4 — 11.8
Painting White, Drabs &c 185 yds e 1 — 9.5.0
do do 414 ft Base 2 — 3.9.0
do do 54 do e 3½ — 15.9
do in Kitchen Porch &c 93 yds e 7½ — 2.18.1½
do do 240 ft Base 1½ — 1.10.—
do & Sanding 32 sills e 1 — 1.12.0
do outside of Windows &c 150 yds e 10 — 6.5.0
do do Green 50 yds e 1/3 — 3.2.6
do Gate &c 30 do e 4 — 10.0
Coloring Walls 165 yds e 4 — 2.15.0
Whitening Ceilings 120 e 2 — 1.0.0
Hanging 13 pieces paper e 1/6 — 19.6
Painting & Marbling & Varnishing Mantle Pieces — 10.0
do & Sanding 4 fireplaces e 1/3 — 5.0
Whitewashing &c in Cellar — 3.9
£ 71.2.6

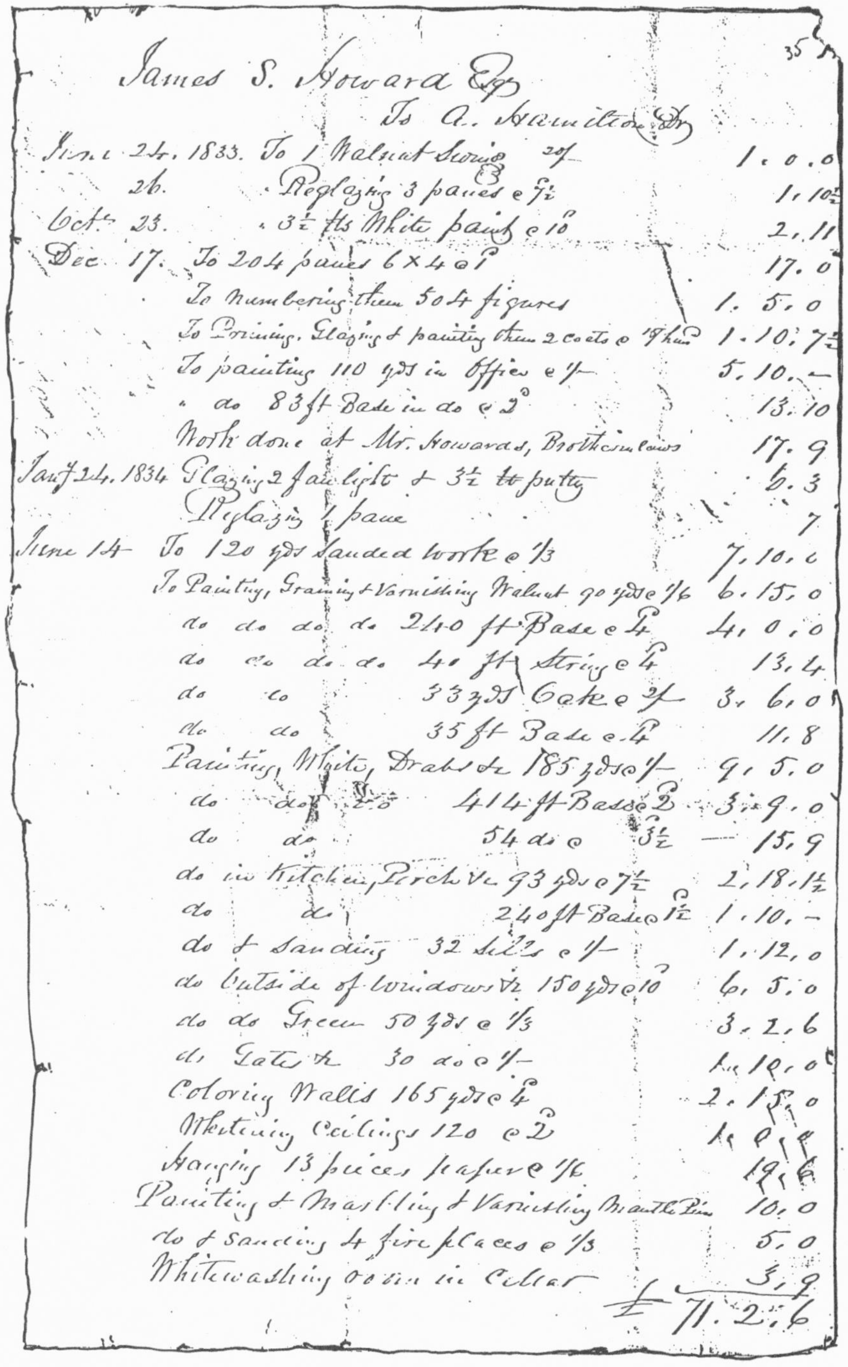

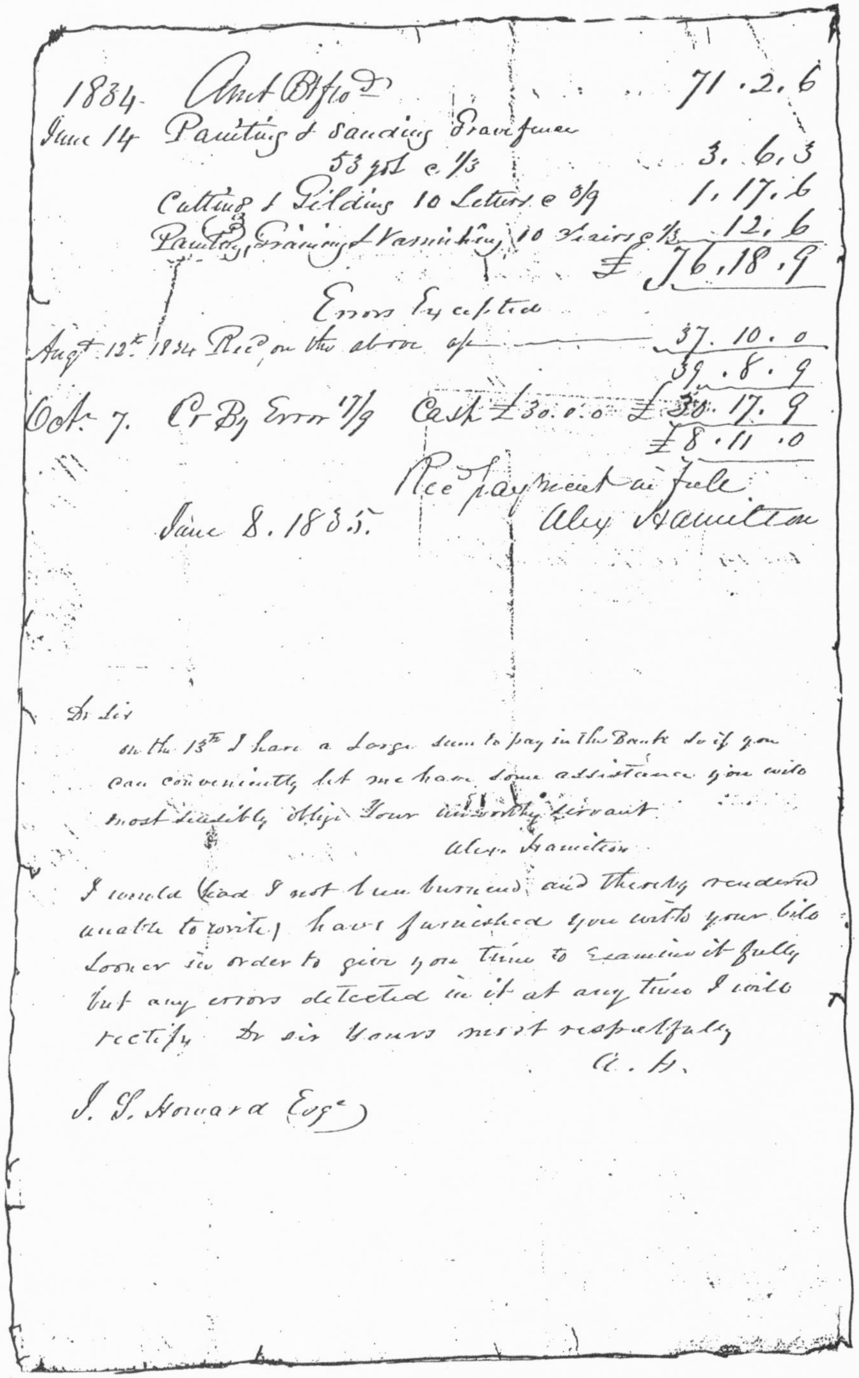

1834 Amt Bt fwd — 71.2.6
June 14 Painting & Sanding Drawfence
53 yds e 1/3 — 3.6.3
Cutting & Gilding 10 Letters e 3/9 — 1.17.6
Painting Graining & Varnishing 10 Stairs e 1/3 — 12.6
£ 76.18.9

Errors Excepted

Aug 13th 1834 Recd on the above of — 37.10.0
39.8.9
Oct. 7. Cr By Error 7/9 Cash £30.0.0 £30.17.9
£8.11.0

Recd payment in full
June 8. 1835. Alex Hamilton

Sir
on the 13th I have a large sum to pay in the Bank so if you
can conveniently let me have some assistance you will
most sensibly oblige Your unworthy Servant
Alex Hamilton
I would had I not been burned and thereby rendered
unable to write, have furnished you with your bill
sooner in order to give you time to examine it fully
but any errors detected in it at any time I will
rectify. & Sir Yours most respectfully
A. H.

J. S. Howard Esqr

On April 25th, 1833, Howard completed his purchase of the land for the price of five hundred pounds.(14)

A dividing fence had been installed and the lot cleared of trees by April 22, 1833 by John Harper.(15)

Stayner approved of Howard's new building as well and made suggestions for the efficient operation of his office. "I am pleased to hear you are going to have another office" he wrote, "and hope you will make it a complete one suited to the rising importance of your town; Mr. Macaulay has made an excellent office at Kingston, and you may obtain some useful hints from him. The Buffalo office appeared to me to be very well planned, — perhaps you might manage to run over and look at it."(16)

The original bills for construction of the post office still exist, and tell us that the painting and finishing was completed by Alexander Hamilton, who described himself as a "Gilder &c" and who worked from a shop on "King Street, West of the Jail".(17)

The 83 feet of baseboard installed in the office indicated a public area of about 400 square feet, as did Hamilton's "painting 110 yds in office". The finished office contained a reading room, 204 post boxes — each with a four inch by six inch glass front —as well as a counter with a "Walnut Swing". A fanlight was installed over the door, and the 10 gilded letters spelling "Post Office" were attached outside over the doorway.(18)

The evidence indicates that the post office was opened in December, 1833. According to bills on file in Howard's papers in the Ontario Archives, eight pair of bricks for stove pipes were purchased on September 5, 1833.(19) The *York Directory* of 1833 noted that by October 1, the "New Post Office building" was on Duke Street between The Bank of Upper Canada and "the elegant brick-built mansion of the Honorable Sir William Campbell" although Howard continued to live in and operate his post office on George Street at that date.(20) Alexander Hamilton's bill indicated that most of his finishing and painting for the post office was completed by mid-December, 1833. Howard moved his home and post office before the end of the year. The York Assessment for 1834, "taken in the latter part of 1833" shows J.S. Howard in his brick building on Duke Street with eight fireplaces and one "milch cow". The assessment roll shows as well that Howard was no longer on George Street.(21)

The post office on Duke Street was the fourth and last Town of York post office as well as the first City of Toronto post office after the incorporation of the City of Toronto on March 6, 1834.

Howard and the administration of the Post Office on Duke Street

As the only post office in a city of more than 9,000 people, the Toronto post office was the most important in the province. As the only post office in the provincial capital, Howard's post office provided the postal service for the Government of Upper Canada as well.(22) By 1834, Howard was the most highly paid postmaster in Upper Canada at a salary of £713 for that year.(23)

As the York post office grew in importance, it had also grown in staff. There had been only one assistant in the 1820s. By 1832, Howard's staff had grown to four besides himself; two full time and two part time.(24) By 1837 it had grown to six.

(14) Deed registered in City of Toronto Registry Office, 29 April, 1833 as No. 9792.

(15) *ibid, Business Papers File* No. 4, Folio 24.

(16) T.A. Stayner to J.S. Howard, April 23, 1833, quoted in Howard *op. cit.* p. 19. It is worth nothing that Stayner did not recommend the Montreal Post Office as a precedent. During the same period, the Montreal Post Office was in rented second-storey premises above a row of shops which the Postmaster, Andrew Porteous, regarded as a serious fire hazard. "The Public", Porteous complained to Stayner, "are now obliged to grope up a pair of stairs, hardly any light, and in winter attended with the danger of breaking some of their bones — After getting up they turn into a small lobby half filled with fire wood; an inconvenience we are (for want of room otherwise) obliged to insist upon." Andrew Porteous to T.A. Stayner. January 19, 1835. MG 40 Series "C", Volume 4, pp.488-489, PAC.

(17) *Howard MacLean Papers* loc. cit. Folio 35 (2pp). Statement of Account, owing by James S. Howard, Esq. to A. Hamilton, Esq.,June 8, 1835.

(18) *ibid.*

(19) *ibid* Folio 29.

(20) *York Commercial Directory & Street Guide*, 1833-34. George Walton, editor (Thomas Dalton, York Upper Canada, October, 1833) p.99.

(21) *Assessment Roll for the Town of York for the Year 1834*, Baldwin Room, Metropolitan Toronto Library, original signed by J.G. Beard (1833), copy inscribed "Taken in latter part of 1833, prior to the Incorporation of the City of Toronto. J. Ross Robertson". Printed in *Robertson's Landmarks of Toronto, 1894.* Vol. I, pp.367-376.

(22) See, for example, the correspondence in PAC, Record Group 1E, 15B, Vols. 1-43.

(23) *Journals of the Legislative Assembly - Upper Canada*, Appendix 53, 12th Parliament, Second Session 1836, vol. 1, p.2. According to the same report "the largest gross amount of letter postage in Upper Canada were collected as follows; at (Year 1834)

Toronto	£4,366
Kingston	1,314
Hamilton	582
Brockville	506
Amherstbergh	453
Bytown	395
Belleville	383
London	337
Niagara	330
Prescott	314

(24) *ibid.* p.13. The report lists John Ballard, Junior and B.M. Hayter as permanent assistants and John Ballard and Thomas Nagle as "occasional".

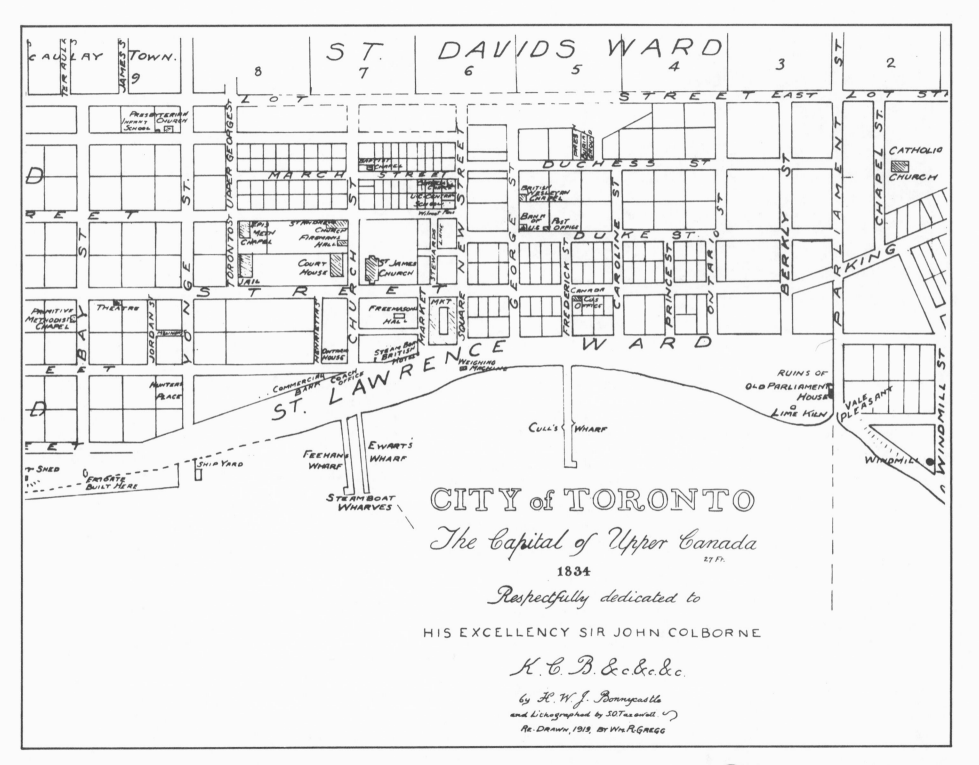

CITY of TORONTO

The Capital of Upper Canada

27 Ft.

1834

Respectfully dedicated to

HIS EXCELLENCY SIR JOHN COLBORNE

K.C.B. &c.&c.&c.

by H.W.J. Bonnycastle
and Lithographed by S.O.Tazewell.
Re-Drawn, 1919, by Wm.R.Gregg

THE ROYAL MAIL

Drawing by C.W. Jefferys
Courtesy Public Archives of Canada

"Now either by way of New-York or Halifax we have a post almost every day."
Anna Brownell Jameson, March 28, 1837

As Postmaster, Howard was responsible for the provision of premises and all capital costs associated with the post office although he was entitled to deduct all costs of the operation, including his commission or salary, from amounts submitted with his quarterly reports to the Deputy Postmaster General in Quebec. As the First Report of the Committee on Finance of the Upper Canada Legislative Assembly put it;

> Mr. Howard, like MacCaulay and every other Postmaster, provides his own clerks, an office, fuel, candles and stationery out of the aggregate sum stated opposite his name.(25)

The Duke Street post office was "open from Eight O'clock A.M. till Seven O'clock P.M. daily, Sundays excepted, on which day it is open from Nine till Ten A.M."(26) Although there were 204 post boxes, Howard carried only 57 monthly accounts at the beginning of 1834, the most important of which were the Government, the Bank and the Indians.(27) In accordance with standard post office procedure, Howard published an advertisement in the local press every three months listing hundreds of Toronto citizens who had mail to pick up.(28) Postage stamps were not in use until the 1850s but each letter was hand cancelled and the amount of postage written on the letter by the Postmaster or his staff.

By the time the post office had moved to Duke Street at the end of 1833, it used only red ink for all mail except the occasional prepaid letter, a characteristic which distinguished it from most other post offices in Upper Canada. This custom originated in 1829, shortly after Howard's appointment as York's Postmaster. "I would be glad" he had written to the Deputy Postmaster General in Quebec, "if it would be possible to get some of the red stuff which they use in Montreal for stamping the letters for at present I have nothing but printers ink, black, and it is such a greasy dirty thing that I would like to be rid of it...".(29)

Howard's clothes were purchased to fit his station. A receipt from tailor Murchison's, at the south-east corner of Duke and George in 1835, confirmed his purchase of a pair of white drill trousers, a "grape gambroon Jacket", a vest and trimmings and an olive frock coat. Ben-

---

(25) *ibid.* The general post office in Quebec, however, provided stationery, forms, locks for mailbags, and cancellation stamps for envelopes. See *Post Office Toronto Records*, loc. cit., Vol. 2.

(26) *City of Toronto Directory*, 1836, p.33.

(27) *Post Office Toronto Records*, loc. cit., Vol. 3.

(28) See, for example, *The Advocate*, York, December 5, 1833, p.4.

(29) *Post Office Toronto Records* 1828-1838, Baldwin Room, Metropolitan Toronto Library, Vol. 2. J.S. Howard to Thos. A. Stayner, Deputy Postmaster General, Quebec, 13 March, 1829.

jamin Hayter, his assistant, purchased a fustian jacket and trousers with a "Valencia Vest".(30)

Howard's caution as a public official was designed to foster the trust of the public. He considered himself a neutral in politics, never voting or even going to public meetings.(31) He was particularly careful in his relationship with William Lyon Mackenzie who was publisher of the *Colonial Advocate*, the most widely read newspaper in the area. Howard felt obliged to place his quarterly advertisements of letters for subscribers to pick up in the Post Office with Mackenzie. Each time, however, Howard wrote for and obtained the instructions of Stayner as his superior officer.(32)

By 1835 Stayner's responsibilities as Deputy Postmaster General had grown to the point where he required a separate assistant or Surveyor for each of Upper and Lower Canada. In April, he first wrote to John Macaulay, the Postmaster of Kingston, and offered him the opportunity.(33) When Macaulay refused, Stayner offered the post to James Howard, saying "I consider that you possess all the qualifications that are necessary to the office".(34)

Howard had other plans. In order to provide additional office space in the Duke Street post office, Howard had decided to again move his family. Earlier the same winter, he had purchased a twelve-acre lot on "Gallows Hill", at the rise on the east side of Yonge Street just below the Third Concession, now known as St. Clair Avenue.(35) Howard refused the Surveyor's position and engaged John Richards to build his new house. At the same time Richards was engaged for renovations to the Post Office on Duke Street, including the addition of a "privey", all of which was completed by October 1835.(36) From that time, Howard rode to and from work each day, a return trip of five miles.

Stayner finally turned to Charles Albert Berczy, who had been Postmaster of Amherstburg since 1829, as his third choice for Surveyor. Berczy, (1793-1858) the youngest son of William Von Moll Berczy and Charlotte Berczy, had been born in Niagara. His father,

the first professional architect and painter in Upper Canada had obtained the grant to Markham Township in 1794, then settled 77 German families by 1798, and was thus responsible for forming a settlement of great importance in the early provisioning of York. The elder Berczy, after a disagreement with Lieutenant-Governor Simcoe, had moved to Montreal by 1804 and died in 1813 while on a trip to New York.(37)

Aside from the occasional late delivery, the mails were flowing smoothly by 1837. One Toronto resident, while waiting for mail that might have been late, was still not overly critical: "It is now seven weeks since the date of the last letters from my far distant home. The Archdeacon told me, by way of comfort, that when he came to settle in this country, there was only one mail-post from England in the course of a whole year and it was called, as if in mockery, 'The Express'; now, either by way of New-York or Halifax, we have a post almost every day".(38)

But under the surface the operation of the postal service was a real grievance for the people of the provinces of Upper and Lower Canada. The legislatures of the Canadas had no control over mail, and the excessively burdensome letter rates insured a steady flow of income from the colonies to England. What was worse, the postal rates not only made Thomas Stayner the most highly paid public official in British North America — they also gave him the power to punish newspapers that displeased him. So it was that Mackenzie's *Colonial Advocate* paid the full letter rates on mailed newspapers as it struggled financially. At the same time, the *Montreal Gazette* distributed 2,000 copies of its paper by mail but was required to pay postage for only 250 copies.(39) A committee of the Upper Canada Assembly investigated the Post Office Department in 1836. Not surprisingly it recommended that the post should be taken over by the Assemblies of Upper and Lower Canada.(40)

The routine of Howard's duties in the post office ended abruptly towards the end of 1837.

---

(30) *James Howard Papers*, PAC MG24, B166.

(31) J.S. Howard to T.A. Stayner, 14 February, 1838, *Colonial Office Correspondence*, RG-7 GI Vol. 85 pp.311 & 312.

(32) *Post Office Toronto Records*, loc. cit. Vol. 2.

(33) Stayner to Macaulay, April 28, 1835. *Macaulay Papers*, loc. cit.

(34) Howard to the Earl of Lichfield, 22 February, 1835, *Colonial Office Correspondence*, loc. cit., p.296.

(35) Deed Registered in the City of Toronto Registry Office on 16 May, 1835 as No. 11752 for the County of York.

(36) *Howard (MacLean) Papers*, loc. cit. folio 37, Statement of Account from John Richards, 20 October, 1835.

(37) Firth, *op. cit.*, Vol. I, p. 30n. The Markham population statistic should be compared with the Town of York, which, in 1797, was 241 in total. *ibid*, p. lxxvii.

(38) Anna Brownell Jameson, *Winter Studies and Summer Rambles in Canada*, March 28, 1837 (reprinted by McClelland & Stewart Ltd., 1965) p.70 (first published 1838).

(39) Smith *op. cit.*, pages 196-198, 206-207.

(40) Journal of the Legislative Assembly of Upper Canada, 1836 Appendix 52, *op. cit.*

Nine days in December, 1837

The drama that began the rest of Howard's life opened with the ringing of alarm bells at one o'clock in the morning, on Tuesday, December 5th.(41)

All through the previous day men from the country to the north and west of Toronto had gathered at Montgomery's Tavern on Yonge Street north of the 4th Concession (Eglinton Avenue). By evening they had formed an ill-disciplined military force ready to rebel against the existing authority and to march on Toronto.(42) Before they had had a chance to organize themselves, two loyalists from the city had ridden into their midst, and one of them, Col. Moodie, was shot and killed.

Word of the skirmish reached Toronto quickly and the city and church bells rang the alarm. James S. Howard, at home on Gallows Hill at Yonge Street just below the 3rd Concession (St. Clair Avenue), did not hear the bells.(43) When he arrived at the Post Office early on Tuesday morning, the city was in an uproar. Loyalist troops were massing at the City Hall (which was then at the south-west corner of Jarvis and King Streets) and to add to the chaos, three of his six employees had not reported for work.(44)

At midday, Charles Berczy, the Post Office Surveyor, appeared in the doorway and announced that he had come to stay in the office for a while. He proceeded to examine the mail, opening some letters that appeared suspicious, even though the legality of this action was open to doubt.(45) During the day a guard for the bank was organized, and patrolled in front of the Post Office as well. By evening Howard and his staff took the mail over to the bank which was barricaded with two nine-pound cannons, and left it there for safe keeping.(46) That night, Howard and Berczy slept in the Post Office.

Meanwhile, all had not been well at Howard's home on Gallows Hill. Shortly after noon, Mackenzie and a few of his men broke down

Arrival of Loyalist Volunteers at Parliament Buildings, Toronto, December, 1837

C.W. Jeffreys. Courtesy Public Archives of Canada

---

(41) Baldwin to Quesnel, *Quesnel Papers*, loc. cit., 8 December, 1837.

(42) According to *The Patriot*, 5 December, 1837, page 2, the Rebels were "variously armed". Many of them carried pike poles with heads forged by Samuel Lount, one of the leaders, at his blacksmith's shop at Holland Landing. William Kilbourn, *The Firebrand* (Toronto, Clarke Irwin & Co. Ltd., 1956) p.151.

(43) R.C. Horne, teller at the Bank of Upper Canada, was in bed at his house on Yonge Street just north of the 2nd Concession (Bloor Street). He "did not hear of the alarm or disturbance of the night until I went to town on Tuesday Morning". See R.C. Horne's letter to the *Christian Guardian*, published January 3, 1838.

(44) J.S. Howard to T.A. Stayner, December 14, 1837, *Colonial Office Correspondence*, PAC, RG-7G1, Vol. 85.

(45) Howard to Stayner, December 14, 1837, *ibid.*, p.272. The standard oath of office for postal employees in the 1830s contained a prohibition against opening the mail. The form concluded with the phrase "*This Oath of Office does not authorise any Post-Master or his Assistant to open Letters, unless he have a special authority for that purpose signed by the Deputy Post-Master General*". (Forms for use in Post Offices, 1830s, Public Archives of Canada, MG 24, I 26, Vol. 61). On November 5, 1837, the Government of Lower Canada had ordered the Postmaster at Montreal to submit all letters passing through his Post Office for the examination of the Inspector of Police. Stayner, the Deputy Postmaster General, approved the order, but the Post Master General in England did not consider it until December. There are no available records of any similar order for the Post Office at Toronto. (See *PAC Colonial Office Correspondence*, MG-40, series L, Vol. 7, pp.143-148).

(46) Howard to the Earl of Lichfield, February 22, 1838, *ibid.*, p.297.

Howard's fence. While his men waited on the lawn, Mackenzie entered the house without knocking, and accosted Mrs. Howard. "He wore a great coat buttoned up to the chin", said an eyewitness, "and presented the appearance of being stuffed". He demanded that she provide dinner for fifty men. According to the recollection of Howard's 12-year-old son, Allan, as reported in Dent's *Upper Canada Rebellion*, Mrs. Howard referred Mackenzie to the servant in the kitchen instead of complying with his request. He became furious, shook his horsewhip in her face, "and denouncing the Postmaster to her in most reprehensible terms, he withdrew, and with his forces, moved westward".

Another remarkable, though secondhand, account of the same events, published in *Robertson's Landmarks of Toronto* in 1894, is included in Appendix III. According to this account, the rebels, led by Mackenzie, "captured" Olive Grove, Howard's house on Yonge Street, on December 5, 1837 and used it as a base of operations until December 7, 1837, when they fell back to Montgomery's Tavern.

The tension of imminent attack by the rebels continued unabated in the city on the following day in spite of the news that Sheriff Jarvis and his men had stopped the rebel advance down Yonge Street towards the Bank of Upper Canada building the previous evening in a skirmish at the 1st Concession (College Street). The work load in the post office became even heavier when Herbert Sullivan, one of Howard's three remaining employees, failed to report for work.(47) As on the previous day, the procedures for securing the mail were continued in the bank next door.

On the morning of Thursday, December 7th, Howard's situation took another turn for the worse. As Howard sorted through the morning mail he noticed a letter addressed to himself by John Lesslie, the Postmaster of Dundas. Howard was immediately suspicious. John Lesslie had been partners with William Lyon Mackenzie in a druggist business in York 15 years earlier.(48) Howard had not expected correspondence from Lesslie and took the envelope to Berczy unopened.(49) When Berczy opened it the mystery deepened. Inside was another envelope addressed not to Howard at all but to James Lesslie in Toronto from Joseph Lesslie, the youngest of the Lesslie brothers, in Dundas, written on the evening of December 5th. The letter commented on "the unmilitary-like appearance of a large body of militia" on the wharf at Hamilton, on "the opposition manifested by Sir Fras. B. Head's administration to the just and constitutional right of the People," — and on the "dreadful work which would necessarily devolve upon those men about to embark for Toronto to go out and shoot the Farmers of Yonge Street".(50) According to an affidavit later sworn by Joseph Lesslie, the letter was enclosed in an envelope addressed to James Howard "without his knowledge or consent" because having long known Howard as a friend, Lesslie knew that conditions in Toronto were chaotic and felt that by this method of address, the letter might reach his brother sooner.(51)

Charles Albert Berczy, c. 1850
2nd City of Toronto Postmaster, 1837-1853
Oil painting
Courtesy Consumers Gas Company

(47) Affidavit by Herbert Sullivan, 5 March, 1838,*ibid*, pp.345-346.

(48) Firth, *op. cit.*, Vol. 2, p.82n. There were, in fact, six Lesslie brothers: John, James (1800-1885), George (1804?-1893), Charles, William and Joseph (1813-1904).James was President of the Peoples' Bank in 1837.

(49) Howard to the Earl of Lichfield, 16 March, 1838, *ibid*, p.320.

(50) Affidavit of Joseph Lesslie, 17 March, 1838, *ibid*, pp.328-332.

(51) *ibid*.

On Saturday, December 9th, Ben Hayter, Howard's second clerk, failed to appear for work, suffering from an illness that had progressed throughout the week.(52) Howard was now left with only one employee, his chief clerk John Ballard, junior, even though the work was increasing daily. At 9 o'clock Berczy advised Howard that he was under suspicion of being implicated with the rebels. Howard immediately sat down and wrote a reply to Berczy, formally demanding an investigation if he were to be under suspicion.(53) Howard, sleepless through most of the week, was living a nightmare.

The next day, Sunday, as the Post Office was opened for only one hour in the morning, the bone-numbing load of work eased slightly. Howard was able to ride northward to see his family for an hour on Sunday afternoon, the first time he had seen them since the Rebellion had started.(54)

The pace of work resumed on Monday as Howard, Berczy and the remaining clerk struggled with the piles of mail. His position no more secure than it was on the weekend, Howard heard rumours from some of his well-placed customers that suspicions against him were deepening.(55)

On Wednesday, December 13, 1837, just after the office had opened, Sir Francis Bond Head's secretary appeared and handed Howard a note, stating that "His Excellency the Lieutenant-Governor has thought proper to remove you from the post office at this place."(56)

Howard's prosperity, his life's work diligently built up over 18 years, had been taken from him by a single blow from an arbitrary and autocratic government. There had been no charges against him, no investigation of his conduct — only rumour and an irresponsible exercise of unbridled political power.

That day he retreated to his house on Yonge Street, leaving Charles Berczy in charge of the Post Office.

---

(52) Extract of letter from Moses Hayter, father of Benjamin M. Hayter, to J.S. Howard, 5 March, 1838, *ibid.*, pp.341-344. Ben Hayter died of his illness on March 4, 1838.

(53) Howard to Berczy, December 9, 1837, *ibid.*, pp.275-276.

(54) Howard to Stayner, December 14, 1837, *ibid.*, p.272.

(55) *ibid.* On Sunday, December 10th, Attorney General Hagerman told Berczy that Howard had associated too much with "those people".

(56) John Joseph to J.S. Howard, December 13, 1837, *Colonial Office Correspondence*, R.G. 7, GI, Vol. 85, p.359, PAC.

Government House
13 Dec. 1837.

Sir,

I have it in command to inform you that His Excellency the Lieut. Governor has thought proper to remove you from the Post Office at this place. Mr. Berczy has been directed to take charge of the office for the present.

I have &c &c

(signed) J. Joseph

J. S. Howard Esqr.

Howard appeals for reinstatement

For the next year Howard turned from one official to the next in an attempt to learn the reasons for his dismissal and to be reinstated. At first, Howard had asked Berczy for reasons, but Berczy gave him none, because as he confided to Thomas Stayner, "I am in truth not fully acquainted with them."(57)

Howard then asked Stayner, as his superior officer, for an explanation but was met with the reply that "the Governor considered it incumbent upon him for reasons known to himself to adopt the course he has taken."(58)

By February 1838, when Howard finally secured a copy of Sir Francis Bond Head's letter to Stayner, he found the reasons so vague as to be difficult to answer. The most serious charge was that "as proof that he was confided in by the principal leaders of the Revolutionary Party, Letters were directed to him under a blank Cover to be delivered to persons who were so strongly suspected of Treason as to have been committed for examination during the Rebellion, & one of these Letters, on being opened, was found to contain highly seditious, if not treasonable matter".(59) What was worse, Stayner had written the Postmaster General in England and asked for confirmation of Head's course of action before Howard had a chance to defend himself.(60)

Howard then appealed directly to the Postmaster General in England: "I have no private profession," he wrote "I am 39 years of age, & in fact am ruined unless shielded by the justice of your Lordship".(61)

By May 1838, Sir Francis Bond Head had returned to England after his term of duty in Upper Canada. The more distant he was from the scene, however, the more he was willing to blame Howard for a major role in the rebellion. He recorded that he had dismissed Howard whom he considered "as responsible for the disaffection which notoriously existed not only in his own office at Toronto but which to a most alarming degree characterised the Post Office Department in Upper Canada". "As long as I occupied a post of difficulty and anger," he continued, "I was unavoidably obliged occasionally to strike at those who were most prominent in their efforts to overthrow me...".(62)

The Colonial Secretary, Lord Glenelg, was not convinced by Head's argument. He was, at the same time, unwilling to make a decision that was unacceptable to officials in the Colony and he had Howard's case referred back to the new Lieutenant Governor of Upper Canada, and his Executive Council. Putting it as diplomatically as possible, Glenelg wrote that he was "aware that this case is not without considerable difficulty. The objections charged against Mr. Howard, though sufficient under existing circumstance to justify his removal, may perhaps hardly be susceptible of any very distinct & unequivocal proof."(63)

On June 28, 1838, Howard's appeal was considered by a meeting of the Executive Council consisting of the Lieutenant Governor, Sir George Arthur; William Allan, Howard's former employer in the Post Office, who had only ten years earlier recommended Howard as being "so faithful in all respects"; Robert B. Sullivan, with whom he had emigrated from County Cork in 1819; and Augustus Baldwin.(64)

The Council decided that Howard was not fit to be Postmaster. As he was "not being actually charged with any Crime", the council decided not to recommend an investigation. "For all purposes not connected with the Post Office", they felt, "Mr. Howard has a right to be presumed Innocent until he is proven to be Guilty". But as "there is no way for him to shew his fitness for the situation of Post Master in a time of political excitement and of danger from an Enemy, the trust which would be required to be placed in him must be in the mind and belief of his Superiors in the Department...". The Executive Council noted that "Mr. Howard in private Life was said to associate with persons whose violent course in party politics gave good ground of suspicion of their being connected with the Rebels, or friendly, or at least not adverse to them".

The central feature of the Council's decision not to reinstate James Scott Howard went somewhat further than condemning his passing acquaintance with the rebels. "Previous to the rising in Arms of the

---

(57) Chas. Berczy to Thomas A. Stayner, December 21, 1837, *ibid.*, p.356.

(58) Thos. A. Stayner to J.S. Howard, December 25, 1837, *ibid.*, p.278.

(59) Head to Stayner, January 25, 1838, as quoted in Howard to the Earl of Lichfield, March 16, 1838, *ibid.*, p.319.

(60) Thos. A. Stayner to Howard, January 31, 1838, *ibid.*, pp.238-287. J.S. Howard to Thos. A. Stayner, February 14, 1838, *ibid.*, pp.306-314.

(61) J.S. Howard to the Earl of Lichfield, 16 March, 1838, *ibid.*, p.306.

(62) Sir F. Bond Head to Lord Glenelg, Colonial Secretary, May 13, 1838, *ibid.*, pp.363-369. Stayner privately wrote in a similar vein to the Postmaster General referring to his unsubstantiated "belief that he (Howard) was intimately acquainted with McKenzie and the other Rebels", but that Howard "was cunning enough not to commit himself by open Acts". T.A. Stayner to Lord Lichfield, *private*, April 21, 1838, *ibid.* pp.376-379.

(63) Glenelg to Sir George Arthur, May 29, 1838, *private, ibid.*, pp.488-489.

(64) PAC, RC 7E3, Vol. 36, Reel C-1193. Robert Baldwin Sullivan was, in fact, by the end of 1836 the "Presiding Councillor" of the Executive Council. He was popularly known as "the *Premier* of our Cabinet of Ministers". Jameson, *op. cit.*, p.65. As was the custom, however, Sullivan had been appointed by the Lieutenant Governor. He did not hold a seat in the elected Assembly of Upper Canada.

Rebels near Toronto" the Council's memorandum continued, "there was much reason to suspect that an extensive correspondence had been carried on between the disaffected through Her Majesty's Post Office at Toronto as well as other places...There appears no means of preventing this Correspondence or of discovering the designs of the disaffected but by the establishing a strict surveillance over the Post Office and by causing suspected Letters to be opened and intercepted."

This conclusion, more than any, demonstrated the denial of Howard's right to a fair hearing. The Executive Council decided not to reinstate Howard for a ground that had not even been mentioned before — that Howard had refused to open the mail. As there was no hearing or any charges or even any suggestion of the circumstances of his refusal to open mail, Howard had no ability to know the case against him or to give evidence in rebuttal.

"Although Mr. Howard might have been neutral as regards politics" the memorandum concluded over the signature of R.B. Sullivan, "a man in his situation at least could not be neutral".

Robert B. Sullivan, c. 1837
(1802-1853)

"The *Premier* of our Cabinet of Ministers"
Anna Brownell Jameson, March, 1837

Courtesy Metropolitan Toronto Library Board

When Lord Glenelg heard of the decision of the Upper Canada Executive Council he was surprised at the groundlessness of the reasoning which kept Howard from reinstatement. "I feel bound to acquiesce for the present in the view which you take of this case," he wrote, "But, at the same time, I cannot admit that mere suspicion, though quite a sufficient ground under circumstances of public danger for the removal of a person from a confidential situation, ought to displace him permanently of employment."(65)

In the end, Howard was victim of both the time and the place: the time was during the Rebellion of 1837 and the continued fear of violence that lasted throughout the year 1838; the place was on Duke Street, right next door to the Bank of Upper Canada building. "Robert Sullivan and the rest of the big wigs are getting frightened out of their lives as they dread another Rebellion this winter" wrote Thomas G. Ridout to his wife in October, 1838. "You can hardly imagine the alarm that exists — " he continued, "the Government are employing a number of rascally spies and a most infamous system is established".(66)

Ridout, as cashier or general manager of the Bank of Upper Canada, and as Sullivan's brother-in-law, was in a position to know. The province's gold reserves were stored in the bank building where Ridout lived — not one hundred feet away from the Duke Street Post Office. The bank building had been under guard throughout most of the year. When threats of attack seemed greatest, the Bank Guard was increased to 50 or 60 and barricades set up "so that", in Ridout's words, "we could hold out against anything but artillery — I wish we had a less quantity of gold below in the vault" he commented, "it gives us so much anxiety —and is such an inducement to the rebels —I must try and get it removed to the garrison [at Fort York] as soon as the vault is ready".(67)

By late November, 1838, Robert B. Sullivan, who lived outside of the city, fearing reprisals by the rebels, brought his family and had "taken refuge in the Bank along with me", wrote Ridout.(68)

The ruling establishment could not accept anything but supporters in the vicinity of the Bank of Upper Canada building.

The drama of Howard's dismissal deserves an epilogue.

(65) Glenelg to Sir George Arthur, 24 August, 1838, *Colonial Office Correspondence*, loc. cit., pp.473-475.

(66) T.G. Ridout to Matilda Ridout, October 16, 1838. *Ridout Papers* loc. cit.

(67) *ibid*, November 12, 1828.

(68) *ibid*, November 22, 1838.

Salome MacLean Howard
(1796—1858)
Water colour c.1855

James Scott Howard
(1798 — 1866)
Water colour c.1855

Courtesy Metropolitan Toronto Library Board

(69) *Province of Canada Journals to Legislative Assembly, 1846.* Appendix F, p.4.

(70) Stayner died on June 23, 1868, leaving seven children, his wife Louisa and nine other children having predeceased him. See Mortimer, *op. cit.*, p.742; Stayner's obituary was published in the Toronto *Globe* 25 June, 1868; Stayner's will was dated 4 February, 1868 and probated 25 July, 1868; it is on microfilm at PAO, GS 1967. His son and executor, Sutherland Stayner, lived on Duke Street in what is now called Campbell House. See *Toronto City Directory, 1868.*

(71) *ibid*, Stayner's Dissent refers to "some gentlemen of political influence in Upper Canada" who applied to the Lieutenant Governor to have Howard appointed Post Office Surveyor.

(72) See "John Roaf" by J.M.S. Careless. Article in the *Dictionary of Canadian Biography*, Vol. IX (University of Toronto Press, Toronto, 1976) pp.663-665

(73) See *Colonial Office Correspondence*, R.G.7, G1, Volume 85 Public Archives Canada, pp.370-375.

(74) See the *Examiner*, Toronto, November 4, 1840. Francis Hincks (1807-1885), like Howard, had been born in Cork in Ireland, although, unlike Howard, his family had been of the Irish Presbyterian religion. After a stay in York during the winter of 1830-31, he emigrated with his new wife and settled in York in 1832. He was manager of the Peoples Bank during the 1830s but established the *Examiner* in 1838. Closely associated with Robert Baldwin in politics (they were next door neighbours), he was elected to the Legislature of the new Province of Canada in March, 1841 and was the author of the Great Reform Coalition of English and French Speaking Members of Parliament. He became Prime Minister in 1850-1854 after Baldwin's retirement. Knighted in 1869, he served as Minister of Finance for the Dominion of Canada under Sir John A. Macdonald 1869-1873. After the death of his first wife in 1874, he married the widow of the Honourable Robert Baldwin Sullivan in 1875.

Epilogue

As a result of public dissatisfaction, the Post Office Department in British North America was investigated by a Commission appointed by the Legislature of the Province of Canada in 1840 — an investigation which moved in tandem with the investigation of the system of government just completed by Lord Durham. A majority of the Commissioners reported in February, 1842:

A Department constituted in the manner we have described could scarcely have escaped unpopularity. Power, however purely exercised, if subjected to no popular control and to little check of any kind, will always be liable to suspicion. Concealment creates jealousy and distrust. But if to this we add the fact that from some of the Colonies, the Canadas especially, a large surplus revenue has annually been remitted to England, the public dissatisfaction will appear natural enough....(69)

The third Commissioner, Thomas Allen Stayner, dissented from the majority because he felt the report was a "personal" attack on his administration; that the Post Office, not he himself, was to be the subject of the investigation.

In April 1851, control of the Post Office Department passed from the Postmaster General and Colonial Secretary in England to the Legislature of the Province of Canada.

Thomas Stayner retired to Toronto where he became a director of the Bank of Upper Canada, and its vice-president. He died in Toronto in 1868.(70)

In the Spring of 1839, James Scott Howard sold his house on Yonge Street and moved his family to Trafalgar near Oakville, soon to move again in order to find work. He had taken his case to the people in 1839 with a pamphlet, *A Statement of Facts Relative to the Dismissal of James S. Howard Esq. Late Postmaster of the City of Toronto, U.C.* He did not succeed in winning his reappointment to a position in the Post Office, although he was able to convince many of his peers that he had been wronged.(71)

Two men in particular stood out as his champions. John Roaf, a Congregationalist minister, had come to Toronto from England in October, 1837 just before the Rebellion. (72) Struck by the justice of Howard's case, he was vocal in his support. Early in 1838, he enlisted the support of a British Member of Parliament who wrote to Lord Glenelg on Howard's behalf.(73) Francis Hincks, later Premier of the Province of Canada, was editor and publisher of the Toronto *Examiner* in 1840. On November 4th of that year, he wrote in an editorial that he felt assured that Parliament "will yet procure ample redress for Mr. Howard" but that to have appointed Mr. Howard as commissioner in the Post Office investigation would have done honour to the Government and would have made "some slight reparation to that much injured and truly estimable gentleman".(74)

Finally, in 1842, Howard was appointed Treasurer of the Home District and, after the reorganization of county government in 1849, he became the first Treasurer of York County. He died in Toronto in 1866.

Joseph Lesslie
(1813 - 1904)

The third City of Toronto Postmaster 1853-1879

Thomas Denne Harris
(1803-1873)

Lived in the post office building from 1841-1870

Charles Albert Berczy stayed with his family in the Post Office on Duke Street until the early part of 1839, when he moved the City of Toronto Post Office to the north side of Front Street, just west of Yonge Street. He remained Postmaster of Toronto until 1853. He became the first president of the Consumer's Gas Company, from 1848 to 1856, and was first elected a director of the Bank of Upper Canada in 1840. He died in Toronto in 1858.(75)

After Berczy left the Duke Street Post Office, Howard rented the building to others for a time, then sold it in 1841 to Thomas Denne Harris.(76) Harris was a hardware merchant who had served in the Bank Guard, 1837-38, and had been chief of the Toronto Fire Brigade from 1837 to 1841. He was elected a director of the Bank of Upper Canada in 1860, and continued to live in the Post Office building until 1870. In 1873, the house was sold to the Christian Brothers, who by that time had purchased the Bank of Upper Canada building and converted it for use as the first De La Salle School.(77) Thomas Denne Harris died in Toronto in 1873.(78)

Perhaps the most remarkable sequel was the case of Joseph Lesslie, who in 1837 was named as the cause of Howard's dismissal and who had been described by Sir Francis Bond Head as "a member of a family who...have notoriously been the strongest supporters of Mr. Mackenzie and his doctrines".(79) In 1853, he succeeded Charles Berczy as the fifth Postmaster, a position he held until 1879. He died in Toronto in 1904.

(75) Charles Berczy and his wife Ann Eliza Berczy had one child, a daughter, Charlotte, at the time they lived in the Post Office building on Duke Street. By the time of his death on June 9, 1858, he left eight daughters and one son...all but Charlotte being born after 1843. See instrument registered in the City of Toronto Registry Office on October 15, 1863 at No. 6653. For much of Berczy's biographical information I am indebted to Donna Ivey, Supervisor of Library Services, Consumers Gas Company, Toronto.

(76) Deed registered from James Scott Howard to Thomas Denne Harris, June 12, 1841, as No. 18521, in the City of Toronto Registry Office.

(77) Deed registered from Thomas Denne Harris to the Merchant's Bank of Canada, September 5, 1872, registered as No. 5542A. The property was purchased by the Brothers of the Christian Schools on July 30, 1873 by Instrument No. 7162A.

(78) See J.K. Johnston, "The Social Composition of the Toronto Bank Guards, 1837-38", *Ontario History*, Vol. 64 (1972), p.100

(79) Sir F. Bond Head to Lord Glenelg, May 13, 1831, *Colonial Office Correspondence*, loc. cit., Vol. 85, p.376-379.

Photograph of the residence of Thomas Denne Harris, c.1869
John Ross Robertson Collection, the Baldwin Room
Courtesy Metropolitan Toronto Library Board

De La Salle Institute School, 1872. Courtesy Metropolitan Toronto Library Board

THE DE LA SALLE INSTITUTE

After the collapse of the Bank of Upper Canada, the property at the corner of Duke and George Street was transferred to the government of the Province of Ontario by the bank's trustees.

At the same time, the lot at the corner of Duke and George Streets was being actively considered as the location for a new boys' school by John Joseph Lynch, Roman Catholic Archbishop of Toronto(1) and the Brothers of the Christian Schools.

The Christian Brothers, a Catholic order of teaching brothers founded in 1680 by French aristocrat Jean Baptiste de la Salle, established their first Toronto school, known as the Academy at Jarvis and Lombard Streets in 1851. The Director of the Academy from August 1867 was Brother Arnold of Jesus.

By 1870 the Christian Brothers' Academy had outgrown the frame building it was occupying. On November 29th, Brother Arnold, together with Archbishop Lynch, arranged the purchase of the old Bank of Upper Canada Building for the Christian Brothers from the Ontario government at a cost of $8,000 (2). This was the first real estate the Christian Brothers had owned in the Dominion of Canada.

Archbishop Lynch's role was significant. As Archbishop of Toronto, he made the purchase and then turned over the property to the Christian Brothers, at cost, on the understanding that "if the Brothers should quit the Diocese of Toronto, that property is to revert to the Roman Catholic Episcopal Corporation for the Diocese of Toronto, in Canada."(3)

---

(1) John Joseph Lynch was born in Ireland on February 10, 1816. He was ordained as a Roman Catholic Priest in 1843 and consecrated as Bishop by 1860, becoming Archbishop of Toronto on March 18, 1870. He died on May 12, 1888. See *John Joseph Lynch Papers*, Archdiocese of Toronto Archives.

(2) "History of the District of Toronto, 1880—" Manuscript, p.9, Christian Brothers Provincialate Library, Toronto.

(3) "An agreement between His Grace the Archbishop of Toronto and the Christian Brothers", 30 November, 1879. *Lynch Papers*, loc. cit. A copy of the agreement in the *Lynch Papers* is unsigned and concludes: "the Episcopal Corporation will refund to the Brothers the value of the property and the permanent improvements made from their own savings from the schools or from any other fund belonging to them, but will not refund any money for ordinary expenses and repairs of the house, nor the subscription taken up in the Diocese for the payment of the original purchase".
This agreement, if unamended, would have allowed the Christian Brothers to be reimbursed for any "improvements" to their property, "if the Brothers should quit the Diocese of Toronto".

John Joseph Lynch, D.D.
First Roman Catholic Archbishop of Toronto
Courtesy Archdiocese of Toronto Archives

The Catholic community was elated to have regained the land it sold to Sir William Campbell at least 50 years earlier. "You heard of our splendid purchase and bargain, the Bank Building of Upper Canada", wrote Archbishop Lynch of Toronto to John Walsh, Bishop of London on 3 December, 1870, "we lost 13,000 dollers [sic] by that Bank; but we have regained it. The lot had on it over 50 years ago a small wooden church . . . I thank God from the bottom of my heart for this triumph . . . the bigoted Protestants are simply *enraged* the Catholics jubilant. We blessed this house. It is undergoing repairs, soon to be occupied . . .(4)

Several months later, Archbishop Lynch retold the story of how "some forty years ago that same place belonged to the Catholic Church of this City", but that "the Bank of Upper Canada cast an avaricious eye upon the spot". Now the Catholics had regained it, "a practical proof that Almighty God certainly guides and governs the affairs of men".(5)

The old Bank building was equipped as a boarding school and renamed "the De La Salle Institute". Brother Arnold advertised in the local press that "the spacious building of the Bank — now adapted to educational purposes — the ample and well-devised playing grounds, and the ever refreshing breezes from great Ontario, all concur in making 'De La Salle Institute' whatever its directors could claim for it, or any of its patrons desire".(6)

As the old bank building was not adequate for the foundation of a boys' school on a long term basis, Brother Arnold contracted with Henry Langley, a noted Toronto architect, to build a large addition on the unused portion of the lot lying immediately to the east of the bank's former head office in the early part of 1871. (Langley had been born in Toronto in 1836. His designs included Government House, the residence of the Lieutenant-Governor, in 1868 and the Eighth Post Office at the head of Toronto Street.)(7) A decade of expansion had begun. (See Appendix IV)

During the first week in July, 1871, Brother Arnold organized an event to start raising "an amount ample enough to enable him to work out and complete his grand scheme in the interest of a religious and practical commercial education".(8) Brother Arnold's Bazaar took place on the main floor of the old Bank of Upper Canada building and by all accounts it was a great success. "Hung from the ceilings and along the sides of the immense emporium of merchandise and barter were costly fabrics in every texture", one newspaper reported. "A more suitable place for the holding of the Bazaar could not have been selected". "The taste displayed in its interior arrangement lent the whole affair an air quite Oriental and magnificent".

Henry Langley
(1836 — 1906)

Architect of the De LaSalle Institute, 1871, and the alterations to the Bank of Upper Canada Building and Post Office Building, 1876.

(4) Lynch to Walsh, 3 December, 1870. *Lynch Papers*, loc. cit.

(5) "The La Salle Institute" *The Irish Canadian*, 23 August, 1871 p. 4.

(6) Advertisement dated August 22, 1871, *The Irish Canadian*, Jan. 2, 1872.

(7) Eric Arthur, *Toronto No Mean City* (University of Toronto Press, 1964, 2nd Edition 1974) Appendix A, p. 249. Langley advertised for tenders for excavation in the *Toronto Globe*, July 15, 1871 and for contractors in the *Toronto Globe*, July 28, 1871.

(8) *The Irish Canadian*, 5 July, 1871 p. 4.

Towards the end of August, Archbishop Lynch presided at a ceremony, laying the cornerstone for the addition. According to the newspaper account, "the Archbishop, in a very artistic manner, spread the mortar and struck the stone with the trowel, thus inaugurating a building which, it is hoped, will prove a lasting memorial of the noble efforts being made by the self-denying Christian Brothers". At the end of the evening, "as the large audience were leaving", the Brothers Band played "the patriotic air . . . God Save Ireland".(9)

The new addition, which opened on January 3rd, 1872, was a large three-storey Victorian structure "faced with white brick, with strings and dressings in the same material". A remarkable account of the building describing its original construction and use as well as listing some of the contractors was published in *The Irish Canadian* of December 20th, 1871 and is included in Appendix IV.

The addition was 68 feet wide by 48 feet deep. It consisted of a large basement set aside for a playroom, four large classrooms on the ground floor, a large hall on the second floor with provision for accommodating 500 people; and a dormitory with room for 68 beds on the top floor.

Referring again to Brother Arnold's "grand work", *The Irish Canadian* editorialized that "years and years after Brother Arnold's meek and pure spirit has taken its flight to the Kingdom where toil and care are unknown, those destined to fill our places will point with pride to the noble structure created by his ready hand".(10)

In 1873 the Christian Brothers purchased the "Harris House", the former post office building to the east, and made further renovations to incorporate it with the school in 1876. At the same time the mansard roof was extended to the west adding a third floor to the former Bank of Upper Canada head office.(11)

In 1874 the Brothers had also purchased a back lot to extend the playground and in 1876 they had bought an additional house on George Street and added a portion of its yard to the playground as well.(12)

ANNUAL

Distribution of Premiums

TO THE

STUDENTS

OF THE

DE LA SALLE INSTITUTE,

—IN—

LA SALLE HALL,

—ON—

WEDNESDAY EVENING, JUNE 25, 1873,

AT EIGHT O'CLOCK.

---

(9) *ibid.*, 23 August, 1871, p. 4.

(10) "New Wing to De La Salle Institute", 20 December, 1871, p. 4.

(11) "History of the District of Toronto 1880" loc. cit., p. 9. According to the title, the property was purchased by the Christian Brothers by deed registered on the 30th day of July, 1871 as No. 7109A. The Christian Brothers continued to refer to the post office building as the "Harris House" for the next 25 years.

(12) "History of the District of Toronto", loc. cit., p. 9.

On January 4, 1878, the Christian Brothers community was jolted. "Their much beloved Director, Bro. Arnold, was changed".(13) He had been called suddenly to see his superior in Montreal but "did not know that the call was for a change, therefore the parting with the Brothers and the good people of Toronto was not difficult". The suddenness of his departure caused a sensation that was exaggerated by the delay of any formal confirmation of the change in Directors for more than two weeks.

When the formal announcement was made that Brother Tobias-Josephus was the new Director of the De La Salle Institute, the "annualist" who kept the Christian Brothers' official records took the news stoically: "The change of the beloved Director was taken very quietly", he wrote. "However he may be congratulated on his change, he left a heavy debt of in round numbers fifty-eight thousand ($58,000.00) Dollars on the house. This the good Brother has no more to think of. May his successor succeed in reducing this enormous debt is my sincere wish for him".(14)

Within two years, Brother Arnold's "grand scheme" had brought the Christian Brothers to a halt. According to the Brothers' "Historique", by 1880 "the financial *incubus* under which the house was lying for many years reached a crises [sic] in this year".(15) In spite of increasing enrollments, the Brothers were obliged to discontinue their boarding school, concentrating on the High School with about ninety students. Late in the year, the Christian Brothers made an arrangement with their creditors. By August, 1881, the Christian Brothers had put up their buildings at Duke and George Streets for sale for $50,000.00 and considered ending their teaching in Toronto, leaving the entire job to the Roman Catholic Separate School Board.(16)

In the midst of these difficulties, the Brothers were not left to their own devices. Archbishop Lynch provided the Archdiocese's Solicitor O. A. O'Sullivan to represent the Christian Brothers, their creditors agreed to a 15% reduction in the debt and gave them time to pay. Finally, the other Houses of Christian Brothers across Canada agreed to contribute to pay off the debts. By June, 1882, the balance had been substantially reduced but the situation was never again to be what it had been before.

The Christian Brothers no longer wanted to own the property at Duke and George Streets.(17)

---

(13) *ibid.*, p. 12.

(14) *ibid.*, p. 14.

(15) *ibid.*, pp. 50-51 (emphasis added)
"*Incubus:* 1. an imaginary evil spirit supposed to descend upon sleeping persons; 2. a nightmare; 3. an oppressive or burdensome thing".
The "great incubus" had also weighed down the Bank of Upper Canada in its closing years (*supra*, p. 14) and had undoubtedly afflicted Duncan Kennedy, contractor for the construction of the Bank of Upper Canada Building (*supra*, p. 6). The incubus returned years later during the restoration (see *infra*). For further information, see "Restoring History an Enterprise for 'Lunatic' Heroes" by Leon Whiteson, *Toronto Star*, Sat., May 1, 1982, p. B7.

(16) Brother Tobias, Director De La Salle College to Very Rev. F. P. Rooney, V.G. (Chairman of the Roman Catholic Separate School Board), August 9, 1881. *Lynch Papers*, loc. cit.

(17) "History of the District of Toronto", loc. cit., pp. 50-51.

A page from the Christian Brothers' "Historique"

De La Salle College,
Toronto, Ontario, Canada.
Year of our Lord, 1881.

The annalist had so many other writings to occupy his attention he could not spare time to continue this historique regularly since 1881, and now in 1888, he has to write a mere sketch from memory.

The financial incubus under which the house was lying for many years reached a crises in this year. It was judged prudent not to re-open the boarding school after the summer vacation. The high class of the City Catholic Parochial Schools was transferred to the Institute building in September of this year. The numbers having swelled fast, it was found necessary to open a junior class and also a preparatory class. The Teacher of Drawing, formerly employed to teach the boys of the Institute only, was employed by the School Board to teach all the boys classes of the city.

Late in the year the financial difficulties obliged the Brothers to make an assignment. D.B. Provincial Patricius was present at the meeting of creditors. The creditors decided to give the Brothers three years to pay their debts or to allow a reduction of 15% in case all would be paid within six months.

At a meeting of the Directors of the Brothers houses of Canada, held in Montreal early in December, it was decided to impose a tax on all the houses, and to pay all the debts of the Brothers of Toronto in full. Nearly all the debts were paid in June 1882, except $800 due to D. J. Sadlier, Montreal. When this was paid more than a year later, the firm generously sent back a cheque of $600. During the financial troubles, the director was sued and had to appear in court several times.

In 1884, the Toronto Catholic School Board purchased the Brothers real estate, and the girls High School and St. Michael's School were transferred to the building of the Brothers known as De La Salle Institute.

In 1883, much to the regret of the Brothers of Toronto, the Novitiate, established on Sumach St. in 1880, was closed by a decision of D. B. Provincial Council. The novices were sent to Montreal, and the Director, D. B. Michael was appointed to teach Form II of De La Salle Institute. In January the following year, 1884, D. B. Michael was called to Montreal, very much to the regret of all the Brothers. This withdrawal of a Brother gave much extra toil to the Brothers till a novice was sent in June, in the person of Brother Theobald, to take one of the lower classes.

In March, 1886, Bro. Tobias Josephus, Director, was called to France to make his 30 days retreat at Athis. He had an extended trip through France, Belgium, Holland, England, Wales and Ireland, and visited many schools during his tour. D. B. Odo Baldwin replaced him as Director protempore, and directed the community very well.

The closing exercises every year at the Institute were always very well conducted, and the attendance was always large. The last time our noble Archbishop, Most Rev. J.J. Lynch, presided was in June 1887. Nine students received commercial diplomas.

The awarding of monthly testimonials of merit introduced with some ceremony in September 1887, did very much to promote study.

D. B. Oswald of Jesus who was appointed to teach the II form of the Institute in August 1887, was, very much to the regret of the entire community, called to be Director of St. Patrick's, Quebec, in December to replace the late lamented Bro. Martin John, formerly of this community.

In the present year, the beatification

The De La Salle Building, c. 1909
Courtesy Metropolitan Toronto Library Board

THE ROMAN CATHOLIC
SEPARATE SCHOOL BOARD

Monsignore Francis Patrick Rooney, Vicar General (1822-1894) Chairman of the Toronto Roman Catholic Separate School Board 1879-1893.

By the end of 1882, the Catholic schools in the central area of Toronto had an enrollment of about 600 students. Ninety of these were in the High School being run by the Christian Brothers in the De La Salle Institute. The balance went to three small crowded schools on Richmond Street, Jarvis Street and Bond Street run by the Roman Catholic Separate School Board.

In October, 1882, the Chairman of the Separate School Board, The Very Reverend Francis Patrick Rooney, Vicar General, received a letter from J. W. C. Whitney, Estate Agent representing the Christian Brothers.(1) Unless the Board was interested in making a definite offer on the De La Salle Institute, the letter read, Mr. Whitney would offer it elsewhere.

For the next few weeks the issue was debated at a number of special meetings of the Board called to consider the question. The majority of the Board acknowledged that they needed more space and that buying the De La Salle Institute could be the answer. An offer of $25,000.00 was talked of and a committee was struck to talk to the Christian Brothers. The Brothers, to the dismay of the committee, asked $36,000.00 as the price, and the Board, slipping in its resolve, countered with an offer of $20,000.00.(2)

The matter rested for several months with neither side moving.

On July 3, 1883, in a dramatic move, the Archbishop of Toronto, John Joseph Lynch, appeared at a regular meeting of the Separate School Board and asked to speak.(3) He explained that new schools were required immediately to relieve the overcrowding of the schools administered by the Board; that the De La Salle Institute could accommodate 1,000 pupils although there were only ninety using it at the present; that "the Brothers can sell the property at a very good advantage" (it had been appraised at $57,000.00 "by two of the most intelligent real estate agents of the city"), but taking into account that there was "a good deal of the sacred earnings of the Brothers expended on the buildings they wished that the Catholic people should not lose this amount".(4) The Archbishop then announced that the Christian Brothers "had most generously offered to sell the property for $25,000" and that he, the Archbishop, "considered it to be his duty as Chief Pastor of the Catholic Church in this Diocese to help in the pur-

(1) See "Minutes of the Roman Catholic Separate School Board", 1878-1888 (Manuscript) October 6, 1882, p.264. J.W.G. Whitney was quite familiar with the property. He had lived in the 1851 Addition on George Street from 1861 to 1866. (*supra* p.23).

(2) *ibid.*, pp.264-288.

(3) *ibid.*, pp.346-351.

chase of this property for the Catholic people of Toronto". He concluded that "he may be obliged to mortgage the Episcopal Corporation property to assist the Board's present wants, but he will do it willingly".

The Archbishop's proposal was accepted by the Separate School Board at its regular meeting on September 4, 1883 by a vote of 8 to 4, but the bargaining continued.(5) The School Board negotiated the terms of purchase very carefully through its solicitor at a series of meetings with the lawyer for the Archdiocese.

A year later at the opening of school in September, 1884, the Catholic students were still in their old schools and the purchase had not been completed. This, according to the Archbishop, was a "grievous neglect" on the part of the Board. "The excuse" alleged by the Board for not having moved the students to the De La Salle Institute, namely, that the trustees had not yet got their deed to the property from the Archbishop, was "simply childish, to use the mildest possible term".(6)

Undaunted, the trustees agreed that repairs to the De La Salle Institute "be proceeded with immediately or as soon as possible after the deeds of said property have been obtained".(7)

On November 7, 1884, the Separate School Board agreed to budget $8,500.00 for repairs to the De La Salle Institute for providing at once "closets, fences and a new Stair Hall Way, also that the internal arrangements of the Harris House be made, such as raising the ceilings & c in order to have it in keeping with the other building adjoining".(8)

At the same time, it was announced that the Sisters of Notre Dame were anxious to have possession of the Board's present quarters in St. John's Hall on Bond Street.

On December 2, 1884, the Roman Catholic Separate School Board held its first meeting in the De La Salle Institute on the main floor of what had been known as the Bank of Upper Canada Building. The Board had still not got its deed to the property. It proceeded, in any event, to make arrangements for the Girls' High School and St. Michael's School to join the De La Salle High School in the building. The contract for the changing of the floor levels in the post office

building was given to A. Weller at the price of $5,297.00 with an agreement that his work be finished by April 1, 1885.

On 23 December, 1884, the title to the De La Salle Institute was legally transferred to the Roman Catholic Separate School Board.(10) The Christian Brothers' debts had been repaid, and they were about to continue the De La Salle High School rent-free in the De La Salle Institute, now owned by the Separate School Board. Archbishop Lynch had done a service to the Catholic people of Toronto not only by insuring continuity of Catholic education in a location of importance to his adherents, but by making sure that the Archdiocese did not have to reimburse the Christian Brothers for any loss on a sale of their property to outsiders.

The Separate School Board, for its part, had begun a remarkable period where not only its own boardroom and administration, *but all the Catholic students* in Central Toronto, were housed under one roof.

The "Novitiate"

Significant changes in the occupancy of the buildings started by the end of 1890.

The credentials of the Christian Brothers as high school teachers had been an issue for many years. Early in 1876 a report on the Separate Schools by a High School Inspector named Buchan had been published in the Toronto *Globe* and had been highly critical of the Brothers. It had highlighted numerous spelling errors in the attendance registers kept by the Brothers and had questioned their capacity as teachers. The issue flared up again at the end of 1877 when the Toronto papers led by *The Evening Telegram* gave publicity to municipal election debates between individuals in the Catholic and Protestant communities as to the adequacy of the Brothers' school.(11)

In a sense, the problem was compounded by the fact that the training of the Brothers as teachers was done in Montreal and that a substantial percentage of the Brothers teaching in Toronto were originally French-speaking. According to the Christian Brothers'

---

(4) The agreement between Archbishop Lynch and the Christian Brothers on November 30, 1870 had used similar language. The Episcopal Corporation was obliged to reimburse the Christian Brothers for their savings spent on improvements, should they decide to quit the Diocese of Toronto. (*supra* p.41).

(5) "Minutes" 1878-1888 loc. cit. pp.355-360

(6) *ibid.*, p.455.

(7) *ibid.*, September 2, 1884, p.457.

(8) *ibid.*, p.469. The "Harris House" was the post office building.

(9) *ibid.*, December 2 and December 4, 1884, pp.472-481.

(10) Deed registered on 23 December, 1884 as No. 4025 SE in the City of Toronto Registry Office.

(11) *History of the District of Toronto 1880* - pp.10-12, Christian Brothers Provincialate Library.

History, "more and more was it seen that there was no use in trying to employ French-Canadian Brothers in the English Schools of Ontario if they had the least French accent. From July, 1879, there were none employed in Toronto to whom any exception could be taken".(12)

Even though there were no more French-speaking Brothers from that date, the Brothers felt that "the prejudice against Brothers trained in the Montreal Novitiate, lasted".

The Brothers opened their own "Novitiate" or teaching academy on Sumach Street in Toronto in 1880 in order to train their own teachers in Ontario. Unfortunately, the experiment was short-lived and closed by 1883 for want of students, among other reasons.

After a reorganization in 1888, the Christian Brothers again decided to open a Toronto Novitiate. This time they made extensive preparations, first enlisting candidates or "Novices", then sending them to the Novitiate in Amawalk, New York for preparation, and finally, preparing premises at the De La Salle Institute in Toronto.(13)

In order to accommodate the Novitiate, the Christian Brothers, in July, 1890, sought permission from the Separate School Board to have the Girls' High School moved from the George Street wing of the De La Salle Institute behind the old bank building to a convent on Bond Street run by the Sisters of St. Joseph. The Trustees of the Board were leaning towards the Brothers' plan until the Sisters in charge of the Girls' High School objected. "They even raised many obstacles to the plans of the Brothers and Trustees", according to the Brothers' account.(14) All through the Fall the Brothers worked "to gain their point with the Trustees", and finally succeeded with the assistance of Archbishop Walsh of Toronto, and Very Reverend Father Rooney, Chairman of the Separate School Board.

On the first Tuesday in December, 1890, the Board decided to allow the Christian Brothers to have the Girls' High School moved so that the Novitiate could replace it. The Brothers were required to pay the High School's expenses of renovating the Bond Street convent, as well as a rent of $200.00 per year for the George Street wing to compensate the Board for rent it would be obliged to pay for the High School at the convent. The Board also allowed the Brothers the use of the De La Salle Hall rent free.(15)

The Brothers completed their renovations to open the Novitiate by December 27. They transformed the "Hall" into "a dormitory, an infirmary and a clothes room and procure combined". The cellar under the George Street wing was transformed into "a very neat refectory", the Brothers moved out the desks from the Girls' High School classrooms and renovated that area as well.(16)

The renovations for the Girls' High School at the Bond Street Convent however, were not going well. According to the Brothers' record, the alterations there "were delayed owing to the bad will of some of the Sisters of St. Joseph who sent away the carpenters". Without knowing the other side of the story, the reasons for the delay may not be clear, but the fact was that the Girls' High School on Bond Street was not ready to be opened when the Christmas vacation ended.(17)

Meanwhile the eleven Novices who were to be the initial students at the Toronto Novitiate were transferred from Amawalk, New York back to Toronto on Saturday, December 26, 1890. They had travelled by train through a record snow storm and arrived, frostbitten, at the De La Salle Institute at 9:00 in the evening, four hours late.(18)

The following day, Sunday, December 27th, was the official opening of the Novitiate. After a mass held by the Archbishop, a morning reception in the Separate School Board Room, and afternoon prayers led by Very Rev. Father Rooney, the program took an unexpected twist.(19)

The Brothers' account of what followed described what must have been the first "sit in" in Toronto's history. In the Brothers' words:

> On the opening day, the Sisters in charge of the Girls' High School marched down with their girls to put the novices out of their rooms. They had not all their own way. Bro. Odo [Baldwin, Deputy Director of the School] met them at the Duke St. door, and allowed them into the Board Room. As soon as his back was turned the headmistress ordered her class into the Brothers' parlour. The Sisters and their girls made no effort to spare the carpet. The blackboard was freely used and the dust did its work in spoiling the parlor furniture. The Novices had to leave their closets free for the Use of the girls.

---

(12) *History of the District of Toronto 1891-94* Introduction p.3, Christian Brothers Provincialate Library.

(13) *ibid.*, pp. 4 and 5

(14) *History of the Novitiate of Toronto from 1890*, p.4, Christian Brothers Provincialate Library.

(15) *History 1891-1894*, pp. 19 and 20.

(16) *ibid.*, p.20.

(17) *ibid.*, p.21.

(18) *History of the Novitiate*, p.7.

(19) *Ibid.*

Bro. Odo, seeing the Sisters were remaining longer than necessary in the Board Room and parlor, got them away the following Monday.

The headmistress all along showed herself everything but a religious or a lady.

The Mother Superior was not against us, but, a weak woman, she was led by her wirepullers.

May they rest in peace. Amen!!.(20)

The Girls' High School "sit in" was thus recorded for posterity. It occurred in an age not noted for its respect for the rights of women. There were no women elected to public office such as, for example, to the Roman Catholic Separate School Board — indeed women were not even allowed to vote. Still the Province of Ontario had passed the Married Women's Property Act just a few years earlier, allowing married women to own property as "persons" distinct from their husbands under the law. The Sisters of St. Joseph and the girls of the High School had blazed a new trail when they marched down to the building at Duke and George Streets to demand their rights — much as had the farmers who marched down to the same building to demand their rights in 1837, many years before.

And in the very same room where the radicals had pressed against the counter and demanded cash for their notes, the girls of the High School sat and waited for their due.

Two years later, the threat of the Girls' High School was again diverted as the Clergy were with the Brothers "to a man". According to the Brother's account:

> In March, 1892, we were informed that the Girl's High School would have to be withdrawn from Notre Dame des Anges Convent, as the Convent would soon be transformed into a hospital. There was danger that we would have to vacate the Novitiate Classrooms. We prayed and worked. Still, there was danger till the last moment. Had we to vacate the rooms, it would have been, perhaps, the dissolution of the Novitiate. Through the kindness and influence of the Archbishop and the clergy, who were with us to a man, we were not disturbed. St. Vincent's Hall

was rented for the High School, and we have still to pay £200 a year for the St. George St. Class-rooms. (21)

And yet somehow, the Sisters triumphed over a time. By the early years of the new century, the Novitiate had closed and the Girls' High School had returned to the De La Salle Institute.

The Twentieth Century — Pre-War Years

By the beginning of the twentieth century, the Separate School Board was looking away from Duke and George Streets for establishing school facilities.

The Board itself moved its meetings from the De La Salle Institute to the New City Hall in about 1900. By 1903, the Board regarded its former boardroom as in "the old building of the De La Salle" and resolved that the floors "which are in a dangerous condition be supported either by columns or beams as per architect's report". (22)

The De La Salle High School ended its 43-year stay in the De La Salle Institute in 1913 when it was moved by the Christian Brothers to 67 Bond Street.

The Novitiate which had started at the end of 1890 and closed several years later, got a new burst of life after a 1906 decision of the Privy Council, that Catholic teachers could have status as employees of a Separate School Board only if they were qualified according to regulations of the Provincial government. In 1907 when the Province of Ontario passed legislation providing for the religious teachers obtaining certificates, provision for a teachers' academy was re-established in the De La Salle Institute. (23) A Junior Novitiate was reopened in 1908, and a Senior Novitiate in November, 1913. The latter event was celebrated by a supper, "served in the Board Room at which 57 in all were present". (24)

The Christian Brothers moved their Novitiate to the new training college they had constructed at Oak Ridges near Aurora in 1916.

From that date, the use of the buildings for educational purposes by the Separate School Board ended.

(20) *History*, 1891-1894, pp. 21-22.

(21) *ibid.*, p.27.

(22) See *Minutes of the Roman Catholic Separate School Board, 1900-1912* loc. cit., p.145, resolution passed April 7, 1903. The Board's Architect for 1903 was W. A. Holmes. *Ibid*, p.134.

(23) *History of the Novitiate*, p.69 ff.

(24) *ibid.*, p.91.

Students sitting on the steps in front of the Separate School Board Room, c. 1900

Courtesy Public Archives of Ontario

The Royal Air Force, Duke Street - Records and Recruiting, c.1918. Courtesy Public Archives of Ontario

The War Years

The Separate School Board continued as owner of the De La Salle Institute which stood empty for two years, notwithstanding the Board's efforts to rent it. (25)

At the beginning of 1918, the Royal Flying Corps and the Royal Naval Air Service were merged into a new Royal Air Force. The Flying Corps and the Naval Air Service had both been prosecuting the aerial war for the British Empire during the Great War. The new Royal Air Force was an attempt to co-ordinate the work of both flying units. As Canada had no independent army or air force, its contribution was as part of the new Royal Air Force.

In July 1918, the Imperial War Munition Board, acting on behalf of the Royal Air Force, rented the De La Salle Building on Duke and George Streets "for a term of two years and for a further term to expire three months after the termination of the war". (26)

According to the agreement, the Imperial War Munition Board was to make improvements at a cost of at least $11,000.00 in accordance with plans and specifications approved by both parties. While there is little evidence of the interior renovations made, a red brick fence was installed along George Street and at the rear of the property in order to enclose the yard. At the same time, the De La Salle stairway to Duke Street was altered so that entry could be gained only from the west side.

The Royal Air Force used the premises for "Records and Recruiting" under the command of Major Hawksford. (27)

As the war had ended in November, 1918, the Royal Air Force surrendered the lease before the end of its two-year term. (28)

From May, 1920, the building was rented to W. C. Cope for a term of five years, although the Board reserved the right to cancel the lease on six months' notice.

The Roman Catholic Separate School Board was looking for a buyer. (29)

---

(25) The buildings were shown as vacant by the assessment rolls. On 7 September, 1915, the Separate School Board had decided "that the matter of producing revenue from the De La Salle building be referred to the Management Committee" *(Roman Catholic Separate School Board Minutes*, 1913-1921, p.175, loc.cit.).

(26) *ibid.*, July 5, 1918, p.343.

(27) *City Directory, 1920*, Toronto Assessment, 28 Duke Street, 1919 for 1920.

(28) Surrender of lease accepted by the Roman Catholic Separate School Board at its meeting on March 25, 1920. See *Minutes 1913-1921*, loc.cit.,p.493.

(29) *ibid.*

Captain, Royal Air Force, 1919

The Christie's Biscuit Building, c.1922
Courtesy of Mike Filey

CHRISTIE'S BISCUITS

The Christie's Building
Corner of Duke and George, May 11, 1923
Courtesy of Mike Filey

In 1874, William Christie and Alexander Brown, carrying on business as wholesale biscuit manufacturers under the name of Christie, Brown & Co. Ltd., built a brick bakery on the south side of Duke Street, across from the east end of the De La Salle Institute. (1)

The firm, which had been established in Toronto in 1853, had grown since its beginning and was to continue to grow on the south side of Duke Street. Additions were built in 1883, 1892, 1899 and 1914 as the company gradually filled up the block between George and Frederick Streets, down to King Street.(2)

In 1914, by the time of its last addition, Christie's had run out of outside space for its employees. Just to the north lay the De La Salle Institute, with its excellent playground —which had been "perhaps the largest in the city" when the Separate School Board had acquired it in 1884.(3) Over the years, the playground had been improved by handball courts and a large hockey rink. As the De La Salle High School had left the previous year, in May, 1914, Christie, Brown & Co. Ltd. applied to the Separate School Board as owner "for use of the De La Salle playgrounds for the Employees during Noon Hour".(4)

When the Separate School Board decided to sell the De La Salle building in 1921, Christie, Brown & Co. Ltd. offered $60,000. The Board accepted the offer on July 5th and the deed was registered on August 11th.(5)

Christie, Brown & Co. Ltd. put their sign on the brick fence on George Street recently constructed for the Royal Air Force, and removed the small iron fence at the front of the buildings.

Apart from using the yard at the rear, Christie's did not occupy the building during the four years of its ownership. Instead, the buildings were subdivided and rented to a large number of commercial and industrial tenants as "the De La Salle Building".

The list includes: the Imperial Oil Co. Ltd. which used the basement of the De La Salle building for making "ESSO" signs; T. W. Langstone, printing; Dominion Brass Products; Acme Paper Bag Co.; Dominion Tobacco Co.; Associated Cigar Makers Ltd.; and Dominion Carbon Brush Co. A full list is included as Appendix V.

Whatever may have been the original intention of Christie, Brown & Co. Ltd. in purchasing the building, they had wound up being involved in a difficult job of property management. Most of the tenants were replaced annually, and by 1925 there were serious vacancies. In the summer of 1925, Christie's put up the De La Salle buildings for sale and sold them at a loss to the United Farmers Co-operative Company Limited.(6)

---

(1) *Toronto City Directories.*

(2) See *City of Toronto Inventory of Buildings of Architectural and Historical Importance* (2nd edition, Toronto Historical Board, April, 1981).

(3) According to Archbishop Lynch, July 3, 1883, *Minutes of the Roman Catholic Separate School Board, 1878-1885,* p. 348, Metropolitan Toronto Separate School Board Archives.

(4) *Minutes of the Roman Catholic Separate School Board, 1913-1921,* loc. cit., p. 73, Meeting of May 5, 1913.

(5) *Minutes of the Roman Catholic Separate School Board, 1921-1922,* loc. cit., p. 33, and deed registered in the City of Toronto Registry Office as No. 499335.

(6) At the price of $57,000.00. Deed registered in the City of Toronto Registry Office on October 1, 1925 as No. 3396ES.

The United Farmers' Building, Duke and George Streets, 1927
Courtesy U.F.C. Archives

"IT BELONGS NOW TO THE MAN BEHIND THE PLOW"

When the Farmers' Co-op completed its purchase from Christie, Brown & Co. Ltd. in the autumn of 1925, they knew that they had bought more than the De La Salle building. They had, in fact, bought the Bank of Upper Canada building — the place where their "ancestors", 90 years earlier, had stood in line demanding cash for their notes in order to force the "Family Compact" to default — the place that had been the object of the march down Yonge Street in December, 1837.

In 1919, a protest vote against the Conservative Government of Ontario resulted in an election where no party had a majority in the Legislature.

The largest group, the "United Farmers of Ontario" with 43 of 111 seats, was more a group than a political party. Only two of its members had had any experience as members of the Legislature. They were obliged to enlist E. C. Drury, who did not hold a seat in the Legislature, to join them as leader and become Premier of Ontario.(1)

The United Farmers of Ontario formed the government until the election of November, 1923 when they were defeated by the Conservatives. But political power was not their main objective. The Farmers were experimenting with co-operative action to better their lot, and after 1923, they turned to marketing.

The United Farmers Co-operative Company Limited, the economic side of the United Farmers of Ontario, had had its office on George Street in a building just north of the former De La Salle buildings from 1922.

The De La Salle buildings were of sufficient size to be used as a headquarters for the organizations as well as a central depot and processing plant for produce sent in by member farmers from all over Ontario.

The second floor of the old Bank of Upper Canada building was converted to a boardroom for the United Farmers of Ontario and the United Farmers Co-operative Company, Limited and the first floor served as offices as well as the editorial office of the Rural Co-operator. The building also became the head office of Co-operative Insurance and was the place of incorporation of scores of co-operatives which functioned throughout Ontario.

United Farmer's Co-operative Board, 1936,
in the Board Room, 2nd. Floor,
Bank of Upper Canada Building
Agnes McPhail standing at left
Courtesy U.F.C. Archives

The United Farmers' Building, Duke and George Streets, c. 1945
Courtesy U.F.C. Archives

Extensive renovations were carried out on the old Post Office building during 1926 at a total cost of $86,000(2). A new mansard roof was added to give additional floor space and the building was turned into a giant cold storage facility. Window openings were bricked in, the building insulated and the up-to-date cold storage system installed.

The balance of the buildings was used as a "central wholesale" with milk and produce brought from member farmers all over Ontario for storage and processing. The buildings also served as the Toronto Creamery Plant, which at one time was responsible for processing a large percentage of the butter used in the City of Toronto.

By 1940 the operations of the "Co-op" required a more efficient elevator. Shortly thereafter the addition at the north end of the buildings along George Street was erected. It provided a good loading dock, a new freight elevator as well as additional storage space.

To the farmers, their new headquarters was not just a building — it was the former Bank of Upper Canada building, the bastion of the ruling Family Compact a century earlier. They saw themselves as the spiritual successors to William Lyon Mackenzie in the epic struggle with the privileged establishment. "It belongs now to the man behind the plow" became their slogan accompanied on their literature by a photograph of the "United Farmers Building, Duke and George Streets"(3), and by the logo of the farmer with his plow.

When the United Farmers Co-operative finally sold its headquarters at Duke and George in 1956, it was not content with a simple notice to the public of its new headquarters. Instead they issued a press release telling an "equal interesting story" of how the United Co-operatives of Ontario were moving *from* 28 Duke Street, Toronto, a building which was significant to them because it was "at one time . . . owned by the Bank of Upper Canada . . . In this building the U.F.O. gained strength"(4).

(1) *Pulling Together for 25 Years*, p.23, Pamphlet in the Ontario Agricultural Museum, Milton, Ontario. E.C. Drury won a seat in the Legislature in a subsequent by-election.

(2) Archives of The United Co-operatives of Ontario, Mississauga, Ontario. Board of Directors Meeting, U.F.C.O. (microfilm) March 18, 1926.

(3) *ibid.*, Document 319, *"Dreams Come True"*. See also for example the following poem attributed to Dr. Herbert H. Hannam, Secretary of U.F.O. and U.F.C.O. from 1933, as it appeared in the same pamphlet:

And its head office housed	Now it stands at the hub
In a building of stone	of a movement that's spreading
That once was a bank,	Like tide at the flood,
Owned by "the few"	As "the many" come into their own.

(4) *ibid.*, Document 108, Huntley W.F. McKay, Director of Information, Ontario Federation of Agriculture to O.R. Evans, Editor, *Family Herald and Weekly Star*, Montreal, July 24, 1956.

December 1979

THE RESTORATION

By 1980, the block at the north-east corner of Adelaide Street East and George Street had become a hulking grey structure, its exterior covered with cement-based paint. Abandoned for seven years while awaiting demolition and development, it had suffered a serious fire on June 30th, 1978.(1)

The roof of the Bank of Upper Canada building had almost completely burned away and was temporarily covered with sheets of plywood. The buildings had been opened to the elements through gaping holes and unprotected window frames. Its exposed woodwork was rotting, its metal covered with rust.

At the same time, the buildings had been designated to be of architectural and historical importance under the Ontario Heritage Act in 1975. In 1979 the National Historic Sites and Monuments Board of Canada declared the Bank of Upper Canada building to be a National Historic Site, a declaration which was followed in February, 1981 by a declaration that the Post Office building was a National Historic Site as well.

Construction started in February, 1980 with the slow and careful removal of debris and interior partitioning of no historic value. By the late spring, the cement-based paint had been removed from the façade to reveal the original stone and brick.

A massive reconstruction of the structural and building systems was required. Entire floors were rebuilt from the ground up. In the De La Salle building alone all 30 structural columns were replaced (although two were reused at other locations in the same block). The roofs were replaced on the bank building and the De La Salle building, and the entire sloping mansard roof was reslated.

Mechanical systems were completely replaced with the most up-to-date equipment including a hydraulic passenger elevator in the De La Salle building and an underground transformer vault for the electrical system. Energy efficiency was made a priority with double-glazed windows throughout and an air-to-air heat pump system for heating and cooling the bank building.

The Post Office building presented the greatest difficulties because of its use as industrial cold storage for over 40 years. The walls and ceilings has been covered with thick sheets of cork in order to insulate the ammonia-charged piping which encircled the walls from floor to ceiling. When the cork was removed and the rot exposed, the entire top floor collapsed and sections of the lower floors had to be replaced as well.

Fire fighters in front of the De La Salle Institute, 1978
Courtesy Toronto Star

(1) "$150,000 Fire Rips Through City Building." *Toronto Star*, Saturday, July 1, 1978, pp. A3 and A4.

"The Hall", De La Salle Institute, December, 1979

The Post Office façade was repaired back to its original appearance with the fortunate discovery of seven thousand matching handmade bricks at a yard in Burlington. Detail for the Post Office restoration was provided by an 1872 photograph, the bills from the original contractor (which had been left in the Ontario Archives), as well as from the remains of the original window sills and lintels still on the inside of the brick wall. Unexpected additional evidence turned up when a complete original Post Office window frame was found encased in the brick wall.

Historical detail which had survived was re-established. Frames and sash were rebuilt for almost two hundred window openings. The decorative iron railing around the portico at the front of the bank building was faithfully reproduced following the drawings filed in the Ontario Archives in 1931.

The first and second floors of the bank building contained a remarkable amount of original woodwork — all in need of repair. The original bank security doors made of pine reinforced with iron rods were still in their original location as were eighteen of the original twenty-three sets of walnut and pine shutters. Mouldings, window casings and baseboards were milled to match sections of the originals which had managed to survive over the century and a half since they were first installed.

Two of the four original Post Office fireplaces were uncovered and again put in working order. The great fireplace in the basement of the bank building was once again made to work — though this required the rebuilding of a sixty-foot chimney. This latter fireplace had served the kitchen of the Ridout family for thirty-five years.

During the course of the restoration, an even more exciting discovery was made in the basement of the Bank of Upper Canada building. While it had been known that the construction of the bank started in 1825, architectural evidence in the basement of the bank building led to the conclusion that the basement had been built at an earlier date. There was, as a result, physical evidence to support the documents which had told of a small building on the "Church lot" many years before.

On the east side of the Post Office, there followed the discovery of a well, made of curved, handmade bricks. The well was repaired, stabilized with mortar, and made the focal point of the landscaping to the east of the buildings.

The project had been undertaken privately with borrowed money. Neither the time for construction nor the budget could be fixed in advance as with more conventional projects, and the funds required for the restoration were borrowed at a floating rate of interest — a prac-

The Restoration: A Personal Scrapbook

PROBLEMS...

CONDITION OF ROOF
AS FOUND, 1979.
NOTE: SKY

TEMPORARY PLYWOOD
ROOF
AS FOUND, 1979

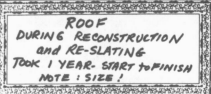

ROOF
DURING RECONSTRUCTION
and RE-SLATING
TOOK 1 YEAR- START TO FINISH
NOTE: SIZE!

tice which may have appeared sound in the early months of 1980. Within a year the "great incubus" returned to haunt the building's owners as the interest rate soared to well over 22% per annum — the highest bank rate in decades. (2)

The restoration was completed by August, 1981, after a construction period of eighteen months. It won the first Credit Foncier Award for the best large-scale private sector restoration in Canada.

In 1982, the project won the Heritage Canada National Award of Honour as the best restoration in Canada, including competition with with government projects.

(2) *Supra*, page 44, footnote (15). A chapter entitled "Guerilla Financing" is not within the scope of this work.

PROBLEMS....

BEFORE: ORIGINAL POST-OFFICE FIREPLACE DISCOVERED 1980.
Post had been built in front of window.

BEFORE: 1980
POST IN FRONT OF ORIGINAL WINDOW OPENING WHICH HAD BEEN BRICKED-IN, 1929.

AFTER: POST REMOVED 1983
REQUIRED STEEL STRUCTURE
Shows Fireplace in First City of Toronto Post Office - re-opened Dec. 15, 1983 as a working post-office.

AFTER: DEC 15, 1983.
POST REMOVED, requiring structural change.
Original 6-over-6 12-LIGHT sash replaced in thermopane. Restored as window in Toronto's First Post Office official opening on its 150th Birthday

PROBLEMS....

BEFORE Landing of Stairway (c.1945) in De La Salle Students' entrance, intersects 1876 arched doorway transom.

BEFORE: Post (c.1925 by U.F.O.) in front of 1851 stairway, discovered hidden in a wall. Used as a cupboard - alternate stairway had been built to the west.

AFTER -1981-
Stairway moved back 8 feet to restore doorway architecture. Now a 3-story-high atrium at entrance door with reproduction gaslights at all 3 window levels.

AFTER: -1981-
Post Removed, requiring major structural change.
1851 Stairway now re-established in its original condition.

PROBLEMS...

BEFORE: INTERIOR SHUTTERS
(1827)
One of 18 pairs (of the original 23 pairs) of walnut and pine shutters as found in 1979 in various conditions and locations. Had many coats of paint; had been cut, re-located and lost.

AFTER: -1981-
INTERIOR SHUTTERS RESTORED after requiring storage and inventory of original locations for safekeeping; several steps of paint removal and restoration; re-establishment of window casings and repair of many damaged shutters.

THE FIRE IN PROGRESS
JUNE 30, 1978
(photograph- George Rust-D'eye)

BEFORE: 1851 DOOR
AS FOUND
(chopped by Fireman's axe, June 30, 1978)
ONE OF 17 exterior doors requiring restoration or renovation.

AFTER: -1981- 1851 DOOR
RESTORED.

NOTE: EARLY VICTORIAN OVAL DOORKNOB.

BEFORE: WINDOW IN "THE HALL"
(second floor De La Salle Building)
AS FOUND - 1979
(ONE OF 150+ WINDOWS REQUIRING REPAIR or REPLACEMENT)

WINDOW "THE HALL" De La Salle
AS FOUND, 1979
LYING "DEAD" ON THE FLOOR
(DAMAGED IN THE FIRE, JUNE 30, 1978)

AFTER: WINDOW IN "THE HALL"
(second floor De La Salle Building)
RESTORED - 1981-
Showing "revived" window.

BANK OF UPPER CANADA

DETAILS OF CAST IRONWORK Plans- c.1931 P.A.O.

Bank of Upper Canada
Woodcut c.1850

1

Portico
When Separate School
Board Headquarters
c.1900

2

Bank Portico As Found 1979
Railing Missing
(Railing had rotted by the 1950's)

3

New Portico Railing Installed
(by Wayne Church)
(May, 1981)

4

Bank of Upper Canada
Portico Restored
Summer, 1983
(landscaping as original)

5

Post Office c. 1834
(from a watercolour by Owen Staples)

1

Post Office Building
c. 1909
as incorporated into the De La Salle Institute in 1876.
NOTE: ARCHED WINDOWS

2

as found - 1979
NOTE: BRICKED-IN ARCHED WINDOWS
(Floor levels, as altered in 1926 by United Farmers making building a cold storage, now intersect windows.)

3

Original 3 Stories of 5 rows of Georgian Post Office Windows Being Reconstructed using sills and lintels of 1833 remaining in the masonry in 1980.
(Matching 9" bricks found in Burlington)

4

NOTE:
These 5 rows of windows provided the clue that this derelict building with its arched windows was actually the 1833 Post Office of James Scott Howard as seen in the Owen Staples drawing (above) found in the Baldwin Room of the Metropolitan Toronto Library, quite by accident, while researching something else!

Post Office Building
Almost Completed.
August, 1981

5

1

3

De La Salle Institute – an addition to the Bank of Upper Canada Building – from an 1872 photo.
NOTE: STAIRWAY AT RIGHT

2

De La Salle Institute
AS FOUND, 1979.

[NOTE: STAIRWAY ABSENT. LOADING DOOR BELOW]

De La Salle Building – during reconstruction of stairway using reinforced concrete – summer, 1980.
[ADELAIDE STREET HAD BEEN WIDENED SINCE 1871, AND DOORWAY HAD TO BE RECESSED TO FORM A REQUIRED LANDING.]

De La Salle Building – Restored, 1981
Once again, used as a school with an "assembly hall" and four classrooms as it was in 1872.

4

The Corner of Adelaide Street East and George Street, 1983

DECEMBER 1983

The buildings at the north-east corner of Adelaide and George Streets are once again fully occupied.

The Bank of Upper Canada building, the 1851 addition and the small addition which had been built by the United Farmer's of Ontario during the period that the buildings served as their head office, is occupied by a firm of nationally known management consultants.

The De La Salle School building is being used in a manner reminiscent of its first use by the De La Salle Institute in 1872, with four classrooms and an assembly hall, again used for examinations.(1)

Most of the Post Office building is used by the Government of Canada. The First City of Toronto Post Office was re-opened as a historical working post office in the oldest surviving post office building in the country on its 150th anniversary in December, 1983 —a project spearheaded through the Town of York Historical Society. The interior of the post office has been restored to the year 1833, depicting the "British period" before the establishment of the Cana-

dian postal service in 1851. Canada Post Corporation has acknowledged that the restoration is authentic and the artifacts in the first City of Toronto Post Office antedate the collection of artifacts in the National Postal Museum in Otttawa. The post office building itself had been declared a National Historic Site in1981 at the request of Canada Post.

Those who participated in the restoration found it to be much more than a construction project. It was, as one journalist put it, "a kind of minor miracle happening down on Adelaide Street."(2) In fact, it could not have happened without the active interest, assistance and advice — most of it voluntary — from a great number of groups and individuals — many of them professional.

The light is on again on the north-east corner of Adelaide and George Streets. This block of buildings is one of the few survivors of more than 150 years of Toronto history. It reaches back tangibly to the beginnings of European settlement in this country in its formative years.

Its continued existence provides a multi-faceted window through which we can begin to understand many of the central events in Ontario's story.

It has now started to fulfill its role in the future.

(1) See article reprinted from *The Irish Canadian*, Appendix IV.

(2) "The Way We Were" by Mike Filey, *The Sunday Sun*, Toronto, December 14, 1980.

APPENDIX I

Typescript copy of specification for completion of
The Bank Building 1827. Original Manuscript in the
Samuel P. Jarvis papers, Metropolitan Library.

Bank Settlement
with
Kennedy Kidd & Co-

Mr. Kennedy being desirous of receiving further advances on account of the Bank contract, which still remains in an unfinished state, the Directors have consented to take possession of the building and making advances under the following conditions-

1- Mr. Kennedy shall leave as a deposit in the Bank the sum of Twenty pounds, as security for his giving the Tin

2- roof of the Bank, (which has been materially injured in the course & progress of carrying up & finishing the Chimney) three coats of paint of dark lead color-having for its comp osition, as a principle indgredient white lead of the best quality and description
and it is understood that previously to the paint being laid on, all fissures or injuries therto, which would occasion leakage, shall be carefully stopped & repaired, with good solder-

3rdly That the wallnut work on the first (floor) should be carefully inspected, & the nail holes should be filled with putty of a proper color & consistency, so as completely to hide the defects-

4 For the completion of the iron railing or Bannister for the front step For pointing & repairing the stone steps-and for repairing the tuck pointing in several parts of the exterior of the building, -and plastering in a proper manner the kitchen porch

5 For plastering & giving them the appearance of Stone resembling the front of the building, the Chimneys from the roof upwards which was done last fall, that have been destroyed by the frost- that work having been performed too late in the season-& it is understood, that the Chimneys are to be completed before the roof be cleaned to receive the paint-
And for any other work which should have been completed under the Contract-

APPENDIX II

The Upper Canada Bank Guard
from the Pay Lists, Canadian Militia, Muster Rolls, 1837-39(Public Archives of Canada MG13, WO13, Vol. 3674)

Officers:

Captain	Ridout, Thomas Gibbs
Lieutenant	Murray, Charles S.
Lieutenant	Anderson, Robert L.
Sergeant	Hinds, William George
Sergeant	Defries, Henry
Corporal	Stow, Alfred
Corporal	Cotton, Henry Calvely to Feb. 28, 1838
	Street, William W. from March 31, 1838

Privates:

Maurice Scollard	Charles Widder
Edward Lefroy Cull	Thomas Dennie Harris
Montague Kelly	Frederick Perkins
John Oliver	Henry Sullivan
William Smith	James G. Armour
John McCullagh	Henry Baldwin Jr.
John Rowe	W.A. Dixie
George Dyett	(Sir) James Robert Gowan
Edward Goldsmith	(Sir) John Hawkins Hagarty
James Hamilton	Edward Hitchings
Thomas J. Leggatt	William G. Loring
William W. Street to March 31, 1838	John Ridout
John Alexander	Charles John Robinson
William Henry Coxwell	Augustus Baldwin Sullivan
John W. Dempsey	(Sir) Adam Wilson
Moore A. Higgins	John C.G. Cochrane
Thomas Collier	Peter H. Howard
(Sir) Thomas Galt	Edward V. Mathias
Donald McDonald	Denis Cornelius O'Brien

CHAPTER CLXXX.

A POPLAR PLAINS HOUSE,

Olive Grove, for Many Years the Residence of Mr. J. S. Howard.

On the Poplar Plains, Yonge st., there stood until recently the building shown in the illustration. It was a noticeable house to the left of the road and lying slightly back, somewhat obscured by fine ornamental trees that overshadowed it. For many years it was the home of Mr. James S. Howard once postmaster of York, afterwards treasurer of the counties of York and Peel, and an active promoter of all works of benevolence. This house used to be known as Olive Grove, and was originally built by Mr. Campbell, proprietor and manager of the Ontario House Hotel in York, a man eminent in the Masonic body and father of Mr. Stedman Campbell, a barrister of note who died early. Mr. Howard died in Toronto in 1866, aged 68 years. During the Mackenzie rebellion this house then occupied by Mr. Howard, was the scene of an incident which is thus related by Samuel Thompson as narrated to him by a gentleman who as a boy was personally cognizant of the facts described. "It was on Monday morning the 5th of December, 1837, when rumours of the disturbance that had broken out in Lower Canada were causing great excitement throughout the home district, that the late James S. Howard's servant man named Boulton, went into his master's room and asked if Mr. Howard had heard shots fired during the night. He replied that he had not, and told his man to go down to the street and find out what was the matter. Boulton returned shortly with the news that a man named Anderson had been shot at the foot of the hill, and his body was now lying in a house near by. Shortly afterwards came the startling report of the death of poor Colonel Moody, which was a great shock to Mrs. Howard who knew him well and was herself a native of Fredericton where the Colonel's regiment, the old Hundred and Fourth, had been raised during the war of 1812. Mr. Howard immediately ordered his carriage and started for the city from whence he did not return for ten days. About nine o'clock a man named Pool who had held the rank of captain in the rebel army, called at Mr. Howard's house and asked if Anderson's body was there. Being told where it was said to be he turned and went away. Immediately afterwards the first detachment of the rebel army came in sight consisting of some fifteen or twenty men, who drew up on the lawn in front of the house. Presently at the word of command they wheeled around and went in search of the dead rebel. Next came three or four men, loyalists, hurrying down the road who said that there were five hundred rebels behind them. Then was heard the report of fire arms and anon more armed men showed themselves along the brow of Gallows Hill and took up ground near the present residence of Mr. Hooper. About eleven o'clock another detachment appeared, headed by a man on a small white horse almost a pony, who proved to be Commander-in-Chief Mackenzie himself. He wore a great-coat buttoned up to the chin and presented the appearance of being stuffed. In talking among themselves they intimated that he had on a great many coats as if to make himself bullet proof. To enable the man on the white pony to enter the lawn, his men wrenched off the fence boards; he entered the house without knocking, took possession of the sitting room where Mrs. and Miss Howard and her brother were sitting, and ordered dinner to be got ready for fifty men. Utterly astonished at such a demand Mrs. Howard said she could do nothing of the kind. After abusing Mrs. Howard for some time, who had incurred his dislike by refusing him special privileges at the post office, Mackenzie said Howard had held his office long enough, and that it was time somebody else had it. Mrs. Howard at length referred him to the servant in the kitchen, which hint he took and went to see about dinner himself. There happened to be a large iron sugar kettle in which was boiling a sheep killed by dogs shortly before. This they emptied and refilled with beef from a barrel in the cellar. A baking of bread just made was also confiscated and cut up by a tall thin man named Eckhart from Markham. While these preparations were going on other men were busy in the tool house mending their arms which consisted of all sorts of weapons from chisels and gouges fixed on poles, to hatchets, knives and guns of all descriptions. About two o'clock there was a regular stampede and the family was left quite alone, much to their relief, with the exception of a young Highland Scotchman mounting guard. He must have been a recent arrival from the old country, as he wore the blue jacket and trousers of the seafaring men of the western island. Mrs. Howard seeing that all the rest had left, went out to speak to him saying that she regretted to see so fine a young Scotchman rebel against his Queen. His answer was, 'Country first, Queen next.' He told her it was the flag of truce which had called his comrades away. About half past three they all returned headed by the Commander in-Chief, who demanded of Mrs. Howard whether the dinner he had ordered was ready. She said it was just as he had left it. Irritated at her coolness he got very angry, shook his horse whip, pulled her from her chair to the window, bidding her look out and be thankful that her own house was not in the same state. He pointed to Dr. Horne's house at Blue Hill on the east side of the road, which during his absence he had set on fire, much to the disappointment of his men whom though very hungry he would not allow to touch any thing but burnt it all up. There was considerable grumbling among the men about it. Poor Lount who was with them, told Mrs. Howard not to

OLIVE GROVE--YONGE STREET.

mind Mackenzie, but to give them all they wanted and they would not harm her. They got through their dinner about dusk and returned to the lawn where they had some barrels of whisky. They kept up a regular or rather irregular firing all night. The family were much alarmed, having only one servant woman with them: the man Boulton had escaped for fear of being taken prisoner by the rebels. There the men remained until Wednesday, when they returned to Montgomery's tavern a mile or so up the road, where is now the village of Eglinton. About eleven o'clock in the morning, the loyalist force marched out to attack the rebels who were posted at the Paul Pry Inn on the east side of the road, with their main body at Montgomery's, some distance further north. It was a very fine sunny day, and the loyalists made a formidable appearance as the sun shone on their bright musket barrels and bayonets. The first shot fired was from the artillery under the command of Captain Craig; it went through the Paul Pry under the eaves and out through the roof. The rebels took to the woods on each side of the road, which at that time went much nearer than at present. Thomas Bell, who had charge of a company of volunteers, said that on the morning of the battle a stranger had asked leave to accompany him. The man wore a long beard and was rumoured to have been one of Napoleon's officers. Mr. Bell saw him take aim at one of the retreating rebels who was crouching behind a stump firing at the loyalists. Nothing could be seen but the top of his head. The stranger fired with fatal effect. The dead man turned out to be a farmer of the name of Wedman from Whitechurch. Montgomery's tavern, a large building on the hill side of the road, was next attacked and quickly evacuated by the flying rebels, who got into the woods and dispersed. It was tnen that Mackenzie made his escape. The tavern having been the rebel headquarters and the place from which Col. Moody was shot, was set on fire and burned down. The house of Gibson, another rebel rendezvous about eight miles up the road, was also burned. With that small effort the rebellion in Upper Canada was crushed. A few days after some fifty or sixty rebel prisoners from about Sharon and Lloydtown were marched down to the city roped together two and two in a long string, and shortly afterwards came a volunteer corps commanded by Colonel's Hill and Dewson raised among the log cabin settlers in the county of Simcoe, came down in sleighs to the city where they did duty all winter. While retreating eastward a party of the rebels attempted to burn the Don bridge, and would have succeeded but for the determined efforts of a Mrs. Ross, who put out the fire at the expense of a bullet in her knee, which was extracted by Dr. Widmer.

APPENDIX IV

The Construction of the De La Salle Institute 1871

TO BUILDERS

Tenders for brick addition to the Institute de la Salle, corner of George and Duke streets, will be received by the undersigned until Wednesday, the 2nd August, at 5 p.m. Plans &c., can be seen at the office of

HENRY LANGLEY, Architect,
Corner of King and Jordan Sts.

TO EXCAVATORS.

Tenders for making the necessary excavation for a new wing to the La Salle Institute will be received up to 5 o'clock on Wednesday evening, the 19th instant.

HENRY LANGLEY,
Architect; corner of King and Jordan sts.

Advertisements in The Toronto Globe by Henry Langley, Architect, calling for tender for the De La Salle Institute, July 1871

The Irish Canadian,
IS PUBLISHED BY
PATRICK BOYLE, - PROPRIETOR,
EVERY WEDNESDAY MORNING,
At the Office, No. 37 Colborne Street,
TORONTO, ONT.

TORONTO, WEDNESDAY, DEC. 20, 1871

NEW WING TO "DE LA SALLE INSTITUTE."

The very handsome addition to De La Salle Institute, which was commenced during the latter part of the past summer, is now approaching completion, and, though economically built, has a bold and imposing appearance. It is situated to the east of, and immediately adjoining the stone building occupied for many years by the Bank of Upper Canada, and which was purchased a short time ago by the Christian Brothers for school purposes, who, finding it too small for their requirements, have erected this new wing in order to supply that want. The structure consists of four stories, including basement and attic—which last is in the Mansard or French roof style. It is contemplated at some future day to extend this roof over the old portion of the building, and, when so executed, it will form a harmonious and extensive group, having a frontage on George street of 77 feet, and 131 feet on Duke st.

The building is faced with white brick, with strings and dressings in the same material. The entrance is approached by a broad flight of steps, which projects about four feet from the main door. This break is carried up to the roof, forming—with its two light semi-circular headed window and large dormer, a central feature. The eaves and deck cornices are executed in galvanized iron, which is a durable and at the same time comparatively inexpensive material. The Mansard roof is covered with slate, having variegated bands between the cornices.

The whole extent of the basement has been set apart for a play-room, and will be used also as a library and reading room. It is well lighted and ventilated and spacious, being 48 feet wide by 63 feet long, with ceiling ten feet high. It is kept well out of the ground, and has an entrance from the play ground and a staircase to the ground floor, which is divided into four large class-rooms, spacious entrance hall and corridor, with doors at the west end opening into the old building, and a staircase at the east end leading up to the assembly room. This room, or hall, is on the first floor, having a ceiling 15 feet high and will seat over 500 people—it will be used for the exhibitions and examinations connected with the school. At the west end is a raised platform, and immediately behind it is a door into the first floor of the old building.

Over the staircase to the hall is another leading to the dormitory in the Mansard roof. This dormitory, which will afford sufficient room for 68 beds, occupies the whole area of the building, is airy and well ventilated, having a ceiling 11 feet 6 inches high. There is also a connection on this floor with the old building, so that in case of fire there will a ready egress in two directions.

The plan of the new wing was designed by Mr. Henry Langley, architect, under whose superintendence it was erected. Messrs. May and Gibbings executed the brick work, Mr. John Wilson the carpentering, Mr. William Redden the plastering, Mr. Rennie the slating, and Mr. Matthew O'Connor the painting and decorating—and creditably have these gentlemen severally fulfilled their contracts.

Christmas vacation commences on tomorrow (Thursday), and will continue till Monday, January 3rd, when the new building will be ready for the reception of pupils. During the interval his Grace the Archbishop of Toronto will bless it—the interesting and solemn ceremony taking place on the last day of the present year, Sunday, the 31st inst.

More enduring than bronze or brass will be this memorial to the unwearied exertion and zeal of the Director of the Christian Brothers' Schools in this city. Years and years after Brother Arnold's meek and pure spirit has taken its flight to the kingdom where toil and care are unknown, those destined to fill our places will point with pride to the noble structure erected by his ready hand, and say, our fathers and mothers aided, more or less, the good disciple of the virtuous and philanthropic La Salle in completing this grand work. And we of to-day but foreshadow the language of posterity in saying that, if his life on this earth was one of sacrifice, of piety and abnegation, his reward in the next will be commensurately great, blissful and eternal.

APPENDIX V

List of Occupants of 28 Duke Street
"De La Salle Building" 1921-1925
from Toronto City Directories

John Schell, Mechanical Expert
John Bresacher, Mechanical Expert
Specialty Sales Co.
Dominion Brass Products
T. W. Langstone Press
Chadwick & Co. Commission Merchants
Dominion Tobacco Co.
Damon Specialty Co.
Dominion Carbon Brush Co.
Electro Mechanical Advertising Co.
MacKay Sales Co.
Kitty Grey's Candy Co.
Standard Silk Shades Ltd.
Johnson & Crook Jewellery Repairs
Adanac Letter Service
Beebe Toffee Mfg. Co. Ltd.
Overall Tire Co. of Canada Ltd.
F. O. Chapman & Co.
Andrew Patterson & Co.
J. B. Mfg. Co.
Nero Mfg. Co.
Display Ad Sales Co.
A.E. Monk Signs
Dr. Dumaurier's Beauty Preparations Ltd.
William Watson, Die Sinker & Engraver
Canadian Plateau Co.
Anna Francis Electroplater
William Watt Ladies Wear
Associated Cigar Makers
Crofton & Crofton Sporting Goods
Arthur Villiers, Piano Tuning and Repairs
Acme Paper Bag Co.
Imperial Oil Limited Advertising Dept. & Carpenter Shop
Delamere and Williams Machinery
Jamieson & Robertson, Asbestos Mfgs.
Tomlinson & Forbes Electric Motor Repairs & Radio Engineer
Dominion Oil Cutout Ltd.
Glover Seed Co.
Silkline Poster Craft

About the Authors

Judy and Sheldon Godfrey

Judy and Sheldon Godfrey, the authors, were also involved in all phases of the restoration of the historical buildings at the "corner of Duke & George Streets".

They had previously won national recognition when they restored a large downtown Toronto historical building in 1978. The restoration, which is the subject of this book, took two years during 1980 and 1982 and was, according to Sheldon, "just about the limit of what ordinary people should be trying to do".

The project won the only two national awards for restoration of heritage buildings — the first Credit Foncier Award in 1981 and the Heritage Canada National Award of Honour in 1982. For their part, the Godfreys were given special recognition by the Toronto Historical Board and earned the nickname of "lunatic heroes" from the Toronto *Star*.

Their work with historical buildings is part of a logical extension of their backgrounds as well as of a commitment to community involvement as the backbone of a democratic society. Sheldon Godfrey is a practising lawyer with a Masters Degree in Canadian History. Judy Godfrey is trained as a physical and occupational therapist who sees her role as "having shifted from rehabilitating people to rehabilitating buildings".

They were both born in Toronto, married since 1961, and are parents of three sons.